Merry Chri...

The
Blue
Cord

God is in the business of making an Extraordinary impact through ordinary Christians. He took uneducated fishermen and turned them into disciples who would take His message around the world. I pray all of us will TRUST God enough to be used by Him for Extraordinary purposes.

♡ Love,
Debbie

Prov. 3:5+6

The
Blue
Cord

Connecting Your Faith With Your Purpose

KAREN BEJJANI

EQUIP PRESS

Colorado Springs

The Blue Cord

First Edition: 2021
The Blue Cord / Karen Bejjani
Paperback ISBN: 978-1-951304-84-3
eBook ISBN: 978-1-951304-85-0
Library of Congress Control Number: 2021922687

EQUIP PRESS
Colorado Springs

Dedication

To my husband, Renod,

without whose love I would never have written this book.

And to the iHOPE community with love and gratitude

for your fellowship on this great adventure.

Our shared experiences inspired this book.

Endorsements

"Am I empathetic? That's not enough. Beyond empathy is compassion. That will get me out of my comfort zone and into God's larger world. This book shows how. Connie, Kate, Jackie, Stephanie, Natasha, and many more nice Christian women were too shy to talk with strangers about anything controversial. But they learned what to say and do, and as a result, Muslim, Buddhist, and Hindu women in America are following Jesus. How did they move friendly conversations forward to focus on Jesus? This book, sprinkled with surprises—sometimes profound and sometimes funny—is filled with practical examples."

—Miriam Adeney, Ph.D.
Associate Professor of World Christian Studies,
Seattle Pacific University
Author of *Daughters of Islam: Building Bridges with Muslim Women*

"Life is challenging and often confusing. We look for signs of assurance and direction yet have forgotten the signs and promises God has already given to us in His Word. In the Bible, the word 'remember' is written five times more than the word 'believe' and two times more than the word 'trust.' Why? Because we forget so easily. God has given us tangible colors, symbols, and signs to remind us of who He is. Don't miss Karen's delightful teaching and personal life journey as she challenges readers to never forget God's promises. You will never look at a blue cord the same again."

—Kathleen Cooke, cofounder of Cooke Media
Group and The Influence Lab
Author of *Hope 4 Today: Stay Connected to God in a Distracted Culture*

"Karen Bejjani has written a refreshing, inspirational, tell-all book that will challenge you to live better for Christ! *The Blue Cord* tells Karen's story, which is the story of most believers and the resident fear they live with in sharing the gospel. Karen was frightened about opening up Jesus conversations, especially with Muslims. But God conquered her fears, and now she has given her life to reaching the people of Islam. The stories are exciting, heartwarming, and even funny at times! The quotes are memorable, and I wrote many of them down to use later. I highly recommend *The Blue Cord*! Great job, Karen, and thank you for challenging us to live our lives with the constant reminder of who Jesus is, who we are, and what we are called to do! Islam is 1/5 of the world now, and they have never been more ready to hear about Jesus than they are today. Find your courage in Christ!"

—**Tom Doyle,** *CEO and Founder of Uncharted Ministries*
Author of *Women Who Risk: Secret Agents for Jesus in the Muslim World*
and *Dreams and Visions: Is Jesus Awakening the Muslim World?*

"Do you have the necessary confidence to share your faith with a Muslim you have just met? Karen Bejjani shows how natural, how loving, and how easy it is to do this very thing. In our multicultural world, we all have the opportunity to rub shoulders with Muslims. This book provides encouragement and thoughtful, practical advice for initiating conversations and relationships across cultural divides. As I write this endorsement, tens of thousands of Afghans are making their way into our neighborhoods. This book will prepare you to love them as Jesus loved by sharing Good News with them."

—**Ted Esler, PhD**
President, Missio Nexus

"Rarely do you find a book that you cannot put down because it captures your heart. This book is certainly a page-turner. From start to finish, you feel like you are looking at Karen's heart through a window. From cover to cover, you will read stories and experiences of real people from many nationalities. These will fill your heart with compassion and love for Muslim people and will challenge you to fearlessly share the gospel with them—being convinced that this is indeed God's purpose for you and all Christians."

—Brother Georges Houssney, Founder & President of Horizons International

Author of *Engaging Islam*

"The migrations of Muslims from the Middle East and North Africa to Western nations have opened the door for Christians to share their faith. But sadly, few Christians reach out to their Muslim neighbors. Bejjani's *Blue Cords* uses a narrative approach to show how "ordinary" Christian women (including converts from Islam) have lived out the biblical principles of compassion, courage, prayer, and witness. Just as the blue cords reminded the ancient Israelites of their obligation to follow God's law, the principles in this book set a standard for how Christians should engage in friendship evangelism."

—Kenneth Nehrbass, Ph.D.

Associate Professor of Global Studies, Liberty University

Author of *The Life and Impact of Phil Parshall: Connecting with Muslims*

"Karen Bejani's book titled *The Blue Cord* is many things—challenging, informative, an easy read, and directed to women (although men will be blessed by reading it)."

"Challenging – Most of us who follow Christ rarely share our faith. Maybe if someone asks a question, but we are not constantly on the lookout for an opportunity or an opening. I am sure when we get to heaven, we will never regret the times we did share God's grace but be sorry for the many opportunities we passed by. Fear? Lack of compassion? Not knowing what to say? Karen hits all our reasons."

"Informative – This book showed me ways I can get outside my comfort zone to meet people coming here from countries I will never visit. I can give a little time and effort and be Christ's light. Practical, easy ideas rather than watching a few more hours of Netflix. And they have an eternal impact."

"Easy – If I pray each day for the Lord to open doors, He will. Pray in the morning and quickly ask him to show me missed opportunities in the evening."

"Directed to women – Women in Muslim countries often hold the keys to the spiritual makeup of the family. They are held in the background in their countries but come forward more often in the new freedoms the American culture offers. Sharing with them will bear much fruit."

—Jim West, Cofounder, The Barnabas Group

"Engaging – enlightening – and challenging in a non-intimidating way. If you've ever felt intimidated about sharing your faith, *The Blue Cord* will both inspire and equip you to lovingly share Jesus with your Muslim neighbors and coworkers."

—Laura Woodworth, Developmental Executive,
Cooke Media Group, Author of *Effective Writing:*
Share Your Faith with the World

Contents

Preface

"What are you afraid of? You serve a living God. These people serve a dead god. Why this fear?" Mohammad's heavily accented words pierced my heart, and I winced. He was right. What was I afraid of? I went to the Middle East a good Christian girl, full of grandiose ideas about "reaching the nations for Jesus." Yet once there, I felt only fear when surrounded by a sea of veiled women, men in light blue robes, and mosques bellowing out the Islamic call to prayer. Overwhelming, terrifying fear.

It was a defining moment.

Mohammad's sure, strong belief in the living God magnified my own sickly faith. I'd never shared Jesus with anyone of another faith or culture. To be honest, I had never shared Jesus with anyone. Yet my friend Mohammad, a former Muslim, boldly shared the gospel of Jesus at great personal cost. While living among and witnessing to people who believed radical Islamic ideologies, Mohammad wholeheartedly embraced persecution. He didn't care what people—even terrorists—thought about him when he shared his faith. He cared only about what God thought.

Mohammad radically challenged my thinking. "If they kill me, send ten more believers to share the good news. If they kill those ten, send a hundred. If they kill them, send a thousand. No matter the persecution, even unto death, Jesus is worth it all."

Just like the Apostle Paul, Mohammad was a force to be reckoned with. And God used him as a catalyst to forever change my thoughts and actions about sharing the hope of Jesus. My thoughts went from apathy to fear to curiosity. Along the way, I overcame many faulty assumptions about what it meant to evangelize. While visiting with my new Hindu neighbors in our cul-de-sac one day, it hit me: engaging as an authentic Christian witness had become a lifestyle. I was no longer afraid to share my faith with a woman of another faith. Like Mohammad, I discovered that sharing Jesus is one of the most exciting, rewarding things I *get to do* as a Christian. Now as cofounder of iHOPE Ministries, I spend my days changing the way everyday believers think about sharing their biblical faith with people of other faiths and cultures.

Why Does This Matter?

One day, after praying with a new Muslim friend, she confided, "I've lived in the U.S. for twenty years. You're the first Christian who has ever prayed with me." Her words stung my ears. I had heard this several times from women of other faiths. A Syrian Muslim refugee shared something similar in the Middle East. "Why has no one ever told me about Jesus? I lived and worked among many Christians, but no one ever shared this good news!" Back then, I rationalized this could happen in Syria, especially during the war. But in the United States, where we have the freedom to share our faith? How does this happen here?

My friend's words haunted me. How can a Muslim, Hindu, or Buddhist live in the United States (or any country) for *decades* and never be befriended by a Christian who would point her to Jesus? I knew what stopped me from reaching out. And I wondered, *What is stopping other ordinary Christian women from sharing Jesus? What needs to change for us to step out boldly to share our faith?*

I had a hunch. So I decided to do a series of focus groups with faith-filled Christian women from across the United States and Canada. Their input was fascinating, insightful, and heartbreaking. These women were overwhelmed by the COVID-19 pandemic and struggling to navigate our politically supercharged culture. They so badly want to trust the Lord, to fearlessly share their faith. Yet they shrink back when baited by coworkers who don't believe in God. They were tired of the in-your-face office conversations about what "all Christians" believe about sex, race, or politics. They walk a tightrope every day, trying hard not to offend. One weary focus group participant confided, "It seems as though we Christians are on a losing team."

Ouch. But there is no judgment here because I can relate. In raw, real-life moments like this, we all are prone to forget who God is, who we are, and what we're called to do. Our natural inclination is to pull back, as if everything rested entirely on ourselves—on our own power and words— rather than believing in Almighty God, the author and perfector of our faith.

I could have quickly decided that my sisters-in-Christ didn't have enough faith to share the good news about Jesus, that they lacked moral courage. But it's much bigger than that. They didn't realize the *need* to share their faith with women of other faiths and cultures. It never occurred to them. That resonated with me because I'd felt the same way. Of course, they said they *believed* that women of other faiths and cultures needed Jesus. If you're a Jesus-follower, I'm sure you believe that too. Yet what do your actions say?

What prevented them from crossing religious boundaries to share Jesus? Well, for one, their Christian friends and churches aren't talking about it or being empowered to engage as authentic Christian witnesses with women of other faiths and cultures. Interestingly, most of their local church's many programs empower them to parent, manage their money, and study their Bibles. Yet they fail to take an active role in sharing the hope of Jesus with their neighbors of other faiths and cultures. Isn't this ironic? Jesus told us to go be his witnesses among the nations. And yet we aren't sharing.

This wouldn't have been surprising when the United States was mostly Christian. In the seventies when I was a young girl, 93 percent[1] of Americans identified as Christian. All my neighbors were either Baptists or Methodists. I didn't need to know how to share my faith then unless I planned to be a missionary. Yet now, just 65 percent[2] of Americans identify as Christian. People of many faiths and cultures live among us. We can simply cross the street and reach the nations with the good news of Jesus. And we're not even talking about it.

Something similar happened to the Israelites. After yet another round of disobeying the Lord, he gave his people a physical, visual reminder—a tassel with a *cord of blue* on the hem of their garments (see Numbers 15:37-41). Every time their eye saw it, they would remember who he is, who they were, and what they were called to do.

It's no accident that the Lord gave the Israelites this unique visual reminder—a *cord of blue*. Rich with meaning and purpose, *the blue cord* symbolized his divine commands that they serve a holy, living God. And that their God left instructions for how to remember and trust him.

Just as God sent Mohammad to challenge my apathy and fear, I hope the LORD uses *The Blue Cord* to catalyze you and your believing friends to take an active role in the great commission where you live. Women hold the keys to the faith of the next generation. Together, we can reach them and make major contributions to the spread of the gospel in our generation.

Chapter 1

Who Are You Afraid Of?

"Fear of man will prove to be a snare,
but whoever trusts in the Lord is kept safe."

— PROVERBS 29:25, NIV

"I don't feel very good about this." I checked on his eyes in the rearview mirror. Beads of sweat dripped from his brow, and I realized that he was afraid. In fact, dark foreboding came over me too as we entered this Middle Eastern city. Tears of absolute terror slid down my cheeks. I'd never been so afraid. After a passionate exchange in Arabic with my husband, our driver abruptly parked and left the car idling.

He left us there in the car.

Alone.

Fear lingered in the air.

Men with long, scruffy beards, hair tucked in white turbans, wearing what looked to me like light blue dresses, were walking on the sidewalk beside our car. I could almost touch them. I imagined this is how terrorists looked. I observed one man standing silently on the sidewalk, curiously watching us.

Turning my head slowly, I pretended I didn't see him looking back at me. On the other side of the street were big tanks with guns pointed in my direction. There were no other women like me, no civilians on this street.

My husband Renod and I had planned to meet and encourage Miriam, a courageous Jesus-follower who lived on the outskirts of this city, a place from which most Christians had fled. It was a lonely place for any single Christian female. And it was certainly no place for an ordinary, everyday Christian girl like me to be trembling under her borrowed black hijab, surely about to die a very long way from home.

Seeing me tremble from uncontrollable fear, my husband tried to diffuse the situation. He explained that our driver had inadvertently taken a wrong turn. We were lost in a red-zone neighborhood where radicals had gunned each other down the prior day. Our driver had left the car to get directions.

As he tried to calm me, a man in a blue dress-like robe walked boldly up to our car, bent down, and pressed his face into our passenger-seat window. He peered brazenly into our car. My husband didn't realize this was happening because he was looking at me in the backseat, holding my hand and singing "Jesus loves me" to calm me down.

Assessing the awful situation, I did my best ventriloquist imitation to speak, not moving my lips. "Don't look now, but there's an armed man looking right into your window."

Renod looked over his shoulder at the man, feigning nonchalance. Then he slowly turned back and calmly said, "If he shoots us, this car won't stop the bullets. So I'm going to go out and talk with him now."

What! Who says a thing like that at a time like this? I was still processing the harrowing situation when he stepped out of the car.

My husband had left me in the car, alone, in the Middle East.

The situation was tense. Radical, armed men stood to the right and left of me. The opposing factions had been shooting at one another for days. There's an old saying, "When two dogs are fighting one another, you stay out of the way." Yet there I was smack in the middle of them, and God seemed very far away.

A Reckoning

When you don't walk with Jesus regularly and a crisis comes, it's a moment of reckoning. This was my reckoning. Leading up to this moment, like Martha with Jesus in Bible times, I'd been busy with many things—work, family, smoothing out all the last-minute travel details. In retrospect, they were all the wrong things for this journey. I rode into that dark, oppressive city naïve, exhausted, and spiritually weak. Oh sure, I managed to read a quick devotional every day. Yet I'd be lying if I said I regularly studied my Bible or prayed more than a one-sentence "Lord, help me" prayer.

Now I was feeling all the ramifications. In that critical moment, I couldn't even pray. My brain's neural pathways worked overtime, and I just shut down from stark terror. The rest of the drive to Miriam's apartment was a fog.

Someone guided me into a tiny, ancient elevator in Miriam's apartment building. I practiced deep-breathing exercises to overcome claustrophobia in those tight quarters. The smell of diesel fuel hit my nose. The little elevator slowly, painstakingly, heaved up eight stories. When it finally dumped us out at Miriam's floor, she flung open wide her door, giddy with Holy Spirit joy, and said with a thick English accent, "Welcome to God's house!" Her words were like a tall glass of lemonade on a hot summer day.

She took one look at me, a hot sniveling mess, and assumed control. Circling me in her warm, loving embrace, she ushered me to her tiny kitchen. Then she handed me tissue after tissue after tissue until my hot, awful tears stopped coming and I could breathe again.

"Aren't you afraid?" I asked in wonder.

"No," she answered.

She told me I'd been very brave as she handed me tiny cups of strong-smelling Arabic coffee. Most Jesus-followers had left the city in fear, fleeing conflict. She'd been hungering for the company of other Christians and was glad I'd been brave enough to come. Brave? Ha!

When the call to prayer boomed from the nearby mosque's loudspeaker, it blared through the thin walls of her apartment, rattling the windows. I looked at her wide-eyed with fresh fear. It was the first time I'd heard the Islamic call to prayer in the Middle East, and it unnerved me. She grasped my hand in hers. "Every time I hear that sound, I get down on my knees to pray to my Heavenly Father that He would be glorified here. Let's pray together now, shall we?"

A Stark Contrast

I don't know how you might have handled this situation. I had panicked at the first sight of men in blue dress robes holding guns. The Lord wrecked my good-Christian-girl pride through that terrifying experience. Now I sat with Miriam, clutching her hand with one of mine and holding a pile of used tissues in the other. My eyes were swollen from crying. How could she live in this evil place? I would have been completely worn down from the constant foreboding threat of terrorism. But Miriam spent day after day pouring into women who'd suffered an unimaginable trauma and devastating loss through war. Where did she find the strength and the reserves to love like she did?

Miriam's bold, courageous witness was a beacon of truth in the darkest of places. I'd never met a woman like her. She lived among radical Islamic extremists in a place where warfare could happen at any moment. Bullets might whiz overhead when she walked to her corner market to pick up lemons for a salad, or when she trekked to a prison—going out of her way to pray or study the Bible with the many Muslim women she'd befriended.

"What do you do if the bullets start flying?" I asked in wonder.

"I just stop, drop, and pray. God is always with me."

The pervasive darkness in that city, so full of radical Islamic ideology, had filled me with dread. Yet Miriam was firm and courageous, a steadfast beacon radiating truth. She had seen the worst in people while ministering to women who bore the effects of living amidst war, honor-killings and beheadings. And yet she did not doubt that sharing the good news of Jesus, despite persecution or possible death, was worth it all.

When she shared her story, I was full of wonder and awe. Jesus seemed so close and she knew him so intimately that I imagined I could touch him in her cozy kitchen. I was afraid of the people in this city, yet she felt compelled to love, serve, and point them to the hope and peace that only Jesus brings. I peppered her with a million questions. "How can you so fearlessly share your faith in this adversity? Are you ever afraid? Because sharing your faith could lead to death, do you ever worry about offending someone?"

As she patiently answered each question, I hardly knew what to say. Miriam was not the super-Christian missionary that I thought she was. She was just an ordinary Christian like me. She'd been divorced. She wrestled with pride and anger. She felt lonely and afraid and struggled with what others thought about her. She wondered if she was doing things "the right way." The only difference between her and me was that she didn't waiver in doubt or unbelief about who God is, who she is in him, and what he'd called her to do.

Before meeting Miriam, it never occurred to me to share my faith like she did. If she could do it there, among her radical neighbors, I wondered if I could do it as well. Why had I never thought to share my faith before— especially with women of other faiths and cultures? I'd always thought of myself as a good Christian girl just working and raising a family in the suburbs. I went to church most Sundays, volunteered in the children's ministry, prayed, and did women's Bible studies. I supported several missionaries who went to share the gospel over "there," wherever "there" was.

My believing friends were mostly like me. We were crazy busy working, raising families, doing Bible studies, volunteering. We were overwhelmed and exhausted at day's end. No one I knew had the time or energy to share the hope of Jesus with anyone who wasn't already in our friend circles. We didn't even talk about it.

Isn't it interesting that we didn't talk about it? The irony amazes me. Before Jesus ascended into heaven, he told his disciples, "Go...and make disciples of all the nations (help people learn about me, believe in me, and obey my words)" (Matthew 28:19, AMP). Jesus called us to be witnesses and tell non-believers in our nations and the world the good news of Jesus Christ (see Acts 1:8). Like Miriam, we all should be obediently taking steps to make Jesus known so that "all the earth will be filled with the glory of the Lord" (Numbers 14:21, AMP). And yet neither I nor most Christians I knew were believing or obeying the Lord's command to share our faith, especially with people of other faiths and cultures.

Just a Super-Christian Calling?

In my defense, when I was a kid, 93 percent[3] of Americans identified as Christian. I never had any friends who weren't already Christian. So it's not surprising that sharing the gospel here wasn't a focus. I gave my allowance pennies for an annual missionary fund to support the spread of the good news overseas. Then, as an adult, I supported missionaries in several faraway places. Until I met Miriam, I believed that Jesus' great commission mandate to "go and make disciples of all nations" (Matthew 28:19, NIV) was a special calling for super-Christian missionaries who were going "over there."

Was I the only believer who believed this? I wondered. So I gathered several groups of faith-filled women from across North America to discuss this topic. Remarkably, their experiences were like my own:

"I thought the great commission meant you had to give up everything you owned to go live someplace you would never want to live. And it

would be super hard. I prayed that I wouldn't have to go someplace like that, a place where there'd probably be a lot of snakes."

—Linda

"When I learned about the great commission on flannel boards in Sunday school, I thought it meant you went overseas to be a missionary. I never realized I could share my faith with women of other faiths here. I didn't even realize that was allowed."

—Janet

"I was a young adult when I first heard about the great commission. And my impression was, Oh yeah, it's for those people who are missionaries. It didn't strike me that it was for all of us here."

—Paige

"It wasn't until I met my husband a few years ago that I came to realize that everyday believers should be crossing cultural and religious boundaries to share Jesus here."

—Amy

What are your earliest impressions about what Jesus meant by "go make disciples of all nations?" How has that understanding shaped your Christian witness today? For me, the impression that the great commission was not meant for everyday, ordinary Christians fastened into my subconscious like super-glue well into adulthood.

As the world changed, I didn't notice the mosques, gurdwaras, stupas, and temples multiplying in small towns and big cities across North America. The mainstream churches I attended never talked about reaching these new neighbors for Jesus. There were no classes on how to share my faith, especially with people of other faiths and cultures. Life in my suburban Christian bubble was filled to the brim with raising a family, growing my career, volunteering. I never noticed the growing number of women from other faiths and cultures around me. And it never occurred to me to intentionally seek them out or share the good news of Jesus.

Thoughts and Actions

A wise mentor taught me, "Thoughts lead to actions, and actions lead to results." Knowing that my faith-filled friends and I were completely unaware of our need to be part of the great commission here, how intentional do you think we were in sharing the gospel? Yup, pretty unintentional. The Lord might have been wooing people to himself all around us, and we never noticed. We were focused on raising our families, keeping safe, and pursuing the great American dream. How about you?

It crushes me now to realize that in our generation, the percentage of Americans who identify as Christian has slid dramatically from 93 percent to 65 percent.[4] That's quite a slide. Where I live now in the buckle of America's Bible-belt, just 48 percent[5] identify as Christian. Eight nations are represented in my cul-de-sac alone. Does it trouble you as much as it does me that this rapid decline happened here in our lifetimes? Take a look at these other sobering trends:

- Just 55 percent[6] of Canadians now identify as Christian, and this from a nation founded on biblical principles.
- Only 18 percent[7] of people in Western Europe now identify as a church-going Christian. This is where Protestant Christianity began.
- 55 percent[8] of Americans and 78 percent[9] of Canadians say they haven't shared what it means to be Christian with anyone in months.
- Almost forty years ago, 89 percent[10] of Christians felt they had a responsibility to share their faith. Now, just 64 percent[11] believe this to be true.

- Today, almost *half* of practicing millennial Christians believe it's *wrong* to share their personal beliefs with someone of another faith.[12]

It's ironic. We are free to share our faith here, yet Christianity is declining fast. Meanwhile, in parts of the world where you can be killed for sharing your faith, such as China and Iran, Christianity is growing fast.

Jesus called us to be witnesses and tell non-believers in our suburbs, our nations, and the world the good news of Jesus Christ (see Acts 1:8). We should all be urgently taking steps to make Jesus known so that "all the earth will be filled with the glory of the Lord" (Numbers 14:21, AMP). And yet, most everyday Christians are not believing or obeying the Lord's command to share their faith, especially with people of another faith and culture. What's going on?

Street-Crossing Roadblocks

Why have Christian women in the West been pulling back from sharing our faith even as the Miriams of the world rush in despite persecution? I gathered faith-filled women of all ages from all over North America to find out. Check out the common faith-sharing roadblocks they shared. Which ones resonate with you?

The Unaware

"No one at my church is talking about sharing our faith, especially with women of other faiths or cultures. Do people of other faiths even live here?"

The Tired and Busy

"I've been so busy raising my family to follow Jesus. I don't have time to build a new relationship or share my faith. I'm exhausted

and overwhelmed. Between juggling work, groceries, school, church, parenting, and this [COVID-19] pandemic, I don't have time."

The People Pleaser

"I've definitely held back from sharing my faith because I've been trying to be politically correct. It's hard out there right now. You could say I'm a people-pleaser. I want to be liked, not rejected. And I don't want to offend people or mess things up."

The Unskilled

"The demographics in my neighborhood have dramatically changed. Our new next-door neighbors are Hindu. They just moved here from India. While I am in my backyard reading my Bible in the mornings, I can see my neighbor prostrating to idols in hers. It's daunting even to think about striking up a conversation with her, let alone share Jesus. I don't have the skill-set."

The Ready-to-Start

"I have a few solid, mostly older Christian women friends who actively share their faith. They inspire me. Most are soaked in Scripture and have God's word written on their heart. I know I should be more like them."

As I sat there in the middle of all these rich, deep conversations with my fellow sisters-in-Christ, I couldn't help but think how much we all wanted to trust the Lord and fearlessly share our faith. While we're all struggling to navigate our politically supercharged culture, some are defeated and fatigued from the pandemic. Others are weary from defending themselves from non-believing coworkers who bait them with conversations about what "all Christians" believe about sex, race, or politics. "It's easier to just keep my mouth shut. I'm afraid to offend someone or rock the boat," one young woman sighed. "It feels like we're part of a losing team."

While we seem to have conceded to our own inner monologues and been defensively huddling together doing more churchy things, very few faith-filled women are out in our subdivisions and workplaces sharing the radical, transforming hope of Jesus Christ. Something has gone very wrong.

Remembering

Back in Moses' day, the Israelites were feeling defeated too. To shore up their moral courage, the Lord gave the Israelites a small yet mighty visual reminder—a blue cord—found in an obscure passage in the Old Testament. Every time their eyes fastened on this blue-cord symbol, they were supposed to remember who God is, who they were in him, and what he called them to do—be witnesses in their generation. While many of them ultimately did not embrace what the symbol stood for, all was not lost. That same blue cord quietly wove its way into the New Testament on the hem of Jesus' robe so that you and I might be transformed by the hope and power that comes in his name.

What can you and I glean from this enduring blue cord that might shore up our faith and give us the moral courage to share the hope of Jesus? If you're up for the adventure, I want to invite you to join me in unpacking the meaning and purpose behind this simple blue cord. I'd like to introduce you to ordinary Christian women who've begun living a blue-cord lifestyle. I want you to experience how the blue-cord principles have transformed their faith and witness, then consider how it might change you. I hope you'll imagine with me what can happen when everyday Christian women everywhere begin to embrace their role as blue-cord women and trade their doubt and fear for the moral courage to share their faith.

Think It Through

- What are your earliest impressions of Jesus's command to "go and make disciples of all nations?" (Matthew 28:19-20 NIV).

- How are you seeing Christianity's decline impacting culture?

- What holds you back from sharing your faith?

Chapter Two

The Blue Cord

"If anyone wishes to be My disciple, let him deny himself...
and take up his cross and follow Me."

— MATTHEW 16:24, AMP

The Old Testament book called Numbers describes how God's people refused to take possession of the land that he had already promised them. The Israelites should have been taking God at his word to step into that promised land, yet they balked. Over and over, the Lord patiently reminded them who he was, who they were in him, what he called them to do. Over and over, they said they believed. Yet their actions didn't line up with their words. While God is loving and faithful, he is also holy and can't ignore disrespect and unbelief. So he made the Israelites wander in the wilderness for forty years. They were stuck in an endless cycle of fear, pardon, and rebuke.

At one point, the Lord asked Moses, "How long will (the Israelites) treat me disrespectfully and reject Me? And how long will they not believe in Me, despite all the miraculous signs which I have performed among them?"

(Numbers 14:11, AMP). It's easy to read Numbers and think, *Will they never learn?* And yet, we're a lot like the ancient Israelites, aren't we?

Like the Israelites, many things keep our eyes off the Lord's promises and commands. Sharing Jesus at a time when Christians become increasingly surrounded by a hostile ideology is a struggle. Just like the Israelites, when a coworker makes fun of our faith, or we see people burning Bibles on the evening news, we forget who he is, who we are, and what we are called to do. Our natural inclination is to shrink back, as if everything rested entirely on ourselves—on *our own power and words*—rather than trusting and believing in a holy, living God, the author and perfector of our faith.

A Visual Reminder

The good news is that the Lord knows us intimately and remembers that we are weak—just like he did with the Israelites (see Psalm 103:14). After yet another round of fear, pardon, and rebuke, the Lord gave them a tangible, visual reminder. Every time their eyes saw it, they would remember they were his holy, chosen people and that he expected them to remember and keep his commandments.

Read this passage in Numbers and see if you can find the visual reminder:

> "The LORD said to Moses, 'Speak to the sons of Israel and tell them to make for themselves tassels on the hems of their garments throughout their generations and put a cord of blue on the tassel of each hem. It shall be a tassel for you to look at and remember all the commandments of the LORD, to do them, so that you do not follow after (the desires of) your own heart and eyes... So that you may remember to do all My commandments and be holy (set apart) to your God. I am the LORD your God...."
> (Numbers 15:37-41, AMP)

Did you see it? A tassel with a blue cord on the hem of their garments.

Interestingly, the command is repeated in Deuteronomy, without the added detail, "You shall make yourself tassels on the four corners of the garment with which you cover yourself" (Deuteronomy 22:12, ESV). Detail or not, the significance of these two Old Testament passages is that when God's chosen people looked upon the tassels with the cord of blue, they would remember God's commandments and seek after God's heart, not their own ways.

It's fascinating that the Lord gave the Israelites this visual symbol of his divine commands. "God is a marking, identifying God," writes John Garr, PhD. God often used symbols like the blue cord to direct his people's attention to his Word. Now, why would God do this? Garr observes it's so that the symbol might "awaken in the hearts of his people memories of his great acts of deliverance and to generate faith for his continuing intervention on his behalf."[13]

God knows that humans forget things from generation to generation. He knows that visual symbols help our brains retrieve and remember information. While they didn't know this in Moses' day, scientists today know that our brain's small and mighty visual processor helps us easily remember life experiences. Here's an example. About seven years ago, when I was learning Arabic, I studied for hours only to remember a handful of new words. Eventually, I understood a little of what my Lebanese mother-in-law was saying. Now I can't remember most of those words despite all the hours of study. In contrast, ask me where I was when I kissed my husband for the first time and I can quickly visualize the epic event in great detail. How can I visualize a kiss that happened more than ten years ago without trying, yet not remember a new Arabic word my husband taught me just yesterday? Because God has wired our brains to remember visual symbols like a blue cord. A symbol is more powerful than words.

Now a tassel with a blue cord seems like such an obscure little symbol, yet it's ripe with mind-blowing purpose and meaning that points people right to the heart of God. Let's unpack it together, starting with the hem.

In ancient days, the hem on your clothes was considered an extension of your personal image and authority, much like our cars, jewelry, or fashion would be today. The more important you were, the more elaborate and ornate your hem would be.[14] So when God told all the Israelites to put a tassel on the hem of their clothes, it was significant because it identified every single one of them with nobility.[15] We have this same noble identity today. Peter tells us that we are "a chosen race, a royal priesthood, a holy nation, a people for his own possession, (so that) you may proclaim the excellencies of him who called you out of the darkness into his marvelous light" (1 Peter 2:9, ESV).

According to Jewish custom, four tassels were on the corners of the hem of the people's garments. And each one of those tassels contained eight threads each, seven white threads and one blue. When the Israelites would weave those tassels, they knew that the seven white threads symbolized perfection and purity. And the single blue cord represented God's holiness, his commandments, and what he called them to do.[16]

In ancient Bible days, blue dye was so rare that only the very rich could afford large quantities of it. It was extremely expensive because it was made by extracting tiny amounts of the dye from a rare snail found in one spot just off the coast of the Mediterranean. Yet even the poorest Israelite could afford four blue threads. This rare blue dye was the same color used to make the inner curtain of the Tabernacle (see Exodus 26:1) and the high priest's robes (see Exodus 28:6). This special color blue represented royalty and power, and it's where we get the term "royal blue" today.

Webster defines "royalty" as someone from an elite class who has regal character or bears nobility. Today when we think of royalty, we might think of Queen Elizabeth or the binge-watching series on Netflix called *The Crown* that showcases her reign. That's not the kind of royalty I'm talking about. This blue cord in the tassels on their hem associated everyone—every ordinary Israelite—as noble people who served a holy God.[17]

It fills me with awe to consider that when the Lord told the Israelites to put one blue cord with seven white threads to make four tassels to put on the hem of their clothes, he was giving them a symbol of their identity. The symbol would have been a visible, public witness to other nations and people, too. John Garr says their uniform identified them as "God's army, a force for peace and justice in the earth."[18]

Ponder with me those compulsory tassels on the hem of their garments. Every morning as the Israelites dressed, the symbolic, blue-corded tassels would warn them not to live life in their own way. As their tasseled clothing made them visually stand out among other people, they were reminded to hope in God rather than conform to the world. As they wound and twisted and knotted the symbolic blue-corded tassels, they learned to twist, tie, and bind their lives together with the Lord. This gave them the moral courage needed to fear God, not man.

Touchable

As Christians, you and I are not required to wear a garment with a tasseled cord of blue. The Law of Moses has been fulfilled, and we're covered by the blood of Christ. Modern-day Jews do wrap a prayer shawl called a *tallit* around themselves during prayer. And it contains four tassels, called *tsitsits,* on the corners. Over time, the knowledge of how to make the original blue dye was lost for over a thousand years. Then the dye secret was rediscovered through some enterprising rabbis. Today, a blue cord may or may not be woven into their tassels.

Still, the symbolism of the blue cord doesn't end in the Old Testament. It also makes an appearance in the New Testament. As a faithful, Torah-observant Jew, Jesus would have been a walking, visual reminder that God's people were to remember and keep God's commands rather than follow after their own ways. He would wear tassels with a blue cord on the hem of his robe. And a woman reached out and touched them:

> Then a woman who had suffered from a hemorrhage for twelve years came up and touched the (tassel) fringe of His outer robe; for she had been saying to herself, "If I only touch His outer robe, I will be healed." But Jesus, turning and seeing her said, "Take courage daughter; your (personal trust and confident) faith (in Me) has made you well." And at once the woman was (completely) healed (Matthew 9:20-22, AMP).

Jesus came to earth to be touchable, knowable. This woman knew this. She knew the Great Physician was in her midst. Pushing aside what others thought of her, she made her way through a crowd, her whole soul bent on touching the hem of her Savior's robe for healing. Can you imagine her fingers touching one of the tassels with the cord of blue on Jesus' hem?

The Hope of the World

"Defeatism, fatigue, despair"—this is literally today's news headlines. It's easy to get overwhelmed with so much bad news around us. We know that Jesus saves. Yet when our personal roadblocks get in the way, why is it that we balk when it comes to sharing the hope of Jesus? It's like we've forgotten who God is, who we are in him, and why we're here. It's like we've been asleep. Paul cautioned the church in Rome,

...this is a critical time. It is already the hour for you to awaken from your sleep (of spiritual complacency); ...The night (this present evil age) is almost gone and the day (of Christ's return) is almost here. So let us fling away the works of darkness and put on the (full) armor of light (Romans 13:10-13, AMP).

In my Bible commentary, to "awaken from your sleep" means to wake up from stupid, fatal indifference to eternal things. Here's the thing about stupid, fatal indifference—it's hard to realize that you're being stupid and indifferent until you meet someone who's not. For me, it took going to the other side of the world to realize I was being spiritually complacent. No fellow sister-in-Christ I knew was "flinging away works of darkness." I didn't even have a picture in my mind for what that might look like. My friends and I were all sitting in the church pews, taking Bible studies, and counting it all good. But we definitely weren't suiting up in the whole armor of God and pushing back the darkness of a lost and dying world. No one I knew was even talking about it, let alone doing it.

Then I met some women who intimately knew the Lord, trusted him unconditionally, and embraced being his witnesses. These were ordinary, everyday Christian women who had embraced the blue-cord principles. They knew who they were in Christ. And they were following after him with all their hearts. I think they might inspire you like they inspired me.

Caroline

"Do you know Jesus?" my Syrian refugee friend Caroline asked our Muslim taxi driver in Beirut. "No," he responded. "I don't know him. Who is he?" As I sat in the back seat listening to the two of them talk of deep spiritual things, I kept thinking, *I can't believe she's telling him the good news of Jesus... right now. Here. On this cold, rainy night...in a taxi on the Muslim side of Beirut. Is this even allowed?*

I'd been a church-going believer all my life, and I'd never observed anyone share the good news of Jesus with a stranger—especially a female believer sharing with a Muslim male. Is that possible? Caroline and her family fled the war in Syria with the clothes on their backs. Her father died soon after making the journey. She and her mother didn't have much, yet she did have Jesus. With a profound sense of urgency, she shared the good news like she was giving away water to those dying of thirst.

Miriam

We picked Miriam up from her long international flight, then took her out to eat on the way to our home. After twenty-four hours of travel, she was weary. When our waitress came to take our drink order, Miriam asked her, "Do you know Jesus?" I couldn't believe it. I'd seen her do this in the Middle East. Now she didn't know what time zone she was in, yet she was urgently sharing the gospel of Jesus with our waitress. It was amazing. In just minutes, our waitress was crying and the two of them were talking about deep matters of the heart and what it means to be a Christian. God was not far from our waitress that night because Miriam was there.

Iman

When Iman arrived in America as an international student, she felt a gnawing in the depths of her soul to do more, be better, and try harder so Allah would accept her. Yet no matter how fervently she tried, no matter how many good works she did, it was never enough.

"I could never be good enough to please Allah, so I just quit trying and began living a sinful life," recounts Iman. Decades passed. Iman married and had children. Still, the empty gnawing grew. Iman considered, "It's too late for me to please Allah, yet not for my children." On a whim, she took her kids to a summer neighborhood church program. It was the first time she'd ever entered a church. It was the first time Iman had heard the gospel.

Her impulsive decision to take her kids to church triggered her journey to Jesus.

"I was like a starving beggar who had just found bread. I wanted to share that bread with all the other beggars I knew. That's how I felt when I discovered Jesus. I wanted to share him with everyone."

As a new follower of Jesus, Iman had vivid recurring dreams of sharing her faith with her grandmother in a North African country where it is illegal to share the gospel. She felt the Lord pressing hard on her to go. And yet she held back because she lacked the courage, confidence, and know-how to share her faith with her Muslim family. Plus, she could be killed. "I didn't think I had what it took to share Jesus with my family," Iman confides. Praise God that's not the end of the story. She discovered training and resources from our ministry that helped her skill-up to share her faith.

"My grandmother was ninety-two when I traveled to North Africa to share the hope of Jesus. She accepted him right away. Six months later, she died. Imagine what would have happened if I had not taken that step of faithful obedience. I would not be seeing my grandmother in heaven."

Tatiana

I'm just guessing that you probably don't have to worry about your mother-in-law killing you tonight for being a Christian. Yet Tatiana did. Once she accepted Christ as her Lord and Savior, she faced immediate, life-threatening danger. A "yes" to Jesus in her Islamic-ruled nation is different from a "yes" in North America. Returning home to her devout Muslim family after celebrating her baptism with other believers, she felt like a new woman. She pushed back her headscarf just a bit, then walked out of her bedroom and into the kitchen with newfound freedom. She was thinking, *When I die, I'll go to Jesus. I have absolutely nothing to lose.*

Her devout Muslim family immediately suspected something was different. As they prepared to pray before the meal, she had just seconds to think about how she'd respond. Christ's words burned in her heart: "but whoever denies me before men, I also will deny before my Father who is in heaven" (Matthew 10:33, ESV). She blurted out, "I'm not praying in the name of Allah anymore. I don't believe that he exists. I believe in the name of Jesus. Jesus is my God, not Allah."

Because she had decided to renounce Islam and follow Jesus, her mother-in-law and her husband violently beat her, stabbed her, and left her for dead. Through the paper-thin walls in her home, she could hear her young son crying hysterically after her mother-in-law calmly announced, "Your mother is dead."

Lying in a pool of her own blood, without food or water for three days, Tatiana should have died. But God miraculously intervened and she survived. As a new believer on the run, she faced the death penalty if she got caught. So she went into hiding, right? No. She didn't hide. Guess what she did next.

She went straight into the nearest city and boldly told as many people as she could about Jesus before the authorities could catch her and kill her. She knew the people there needed the peace and hope that only Jesus could bring. Concerned about her safety, believers smuggled her out of her city and into another. There she did the same thing.

Eventually, through a series of stunningly miraculous events, she found her way to America with the clothes on her back and a hundred dollars in her pocket. She's still sharing Jesus with a sense of urgency with as many non-believers as she can. Tatiana lost her child, her family, everything. And she found that Jesus is worth it all.

Counting the Cost

Can you handle it if I give you difficult things to mull over? If so, keep reading.

Unlike Tatiana, you and I have not had to count the cost for our faith. We've not had to wrestle with the privilege of being killed for his sake. My friend knew that her "sufferings of this present life are not worthy to be compared with the glory that is about to be revealed to us and in us" (Romans 8:18 AMP). She believed that Jesus is worth a thousand times the lives of herself and her child. I don't know about you, but I surely didn't have this same level of belief or commitment in Christ. I purposefully ignored the part where following Jesus might include suffering or death.

Whole generations of Americans, Canadians, and Europeans haven't had to deeply weigh a decision for Christ, knowing that we might face communal pressure, shame, or death. We were never purified by fiery trials of persecution like our fellow sisters-in-Christ in China or Iran. Our churches haven't been bulldozed, and our pastors haven't been jailed. Instead, in the spirit of embracing diversity and inclusion, we've become very concerned with pleasing our coworkers, families, friends, neighbors. "You do you. I'll be me. You worship your Hindu gods. I'll worship my Christian God. Let's all just love each other and get along." I've heard things like that a lot. It sounds like the best and most loving thing to do. Yet does it really impart the depth and breadth of what it means to be a Christ-follower?

It's no wonder that many Christians are struggling not to offend coworkers, families, friends, and neighbors with a message that sounds non-inclusive. It seems that as we've embraced comfort and security, we have forgotten that the gospel is a stumbling block to some and offensive to others. Jesus told us, "I am the way, and the truth and the life. No one comes to the Father except through me" (John 14:6, ESV). We are foolish if we think we can be all things to all people and somehow make Christianity popular. Rather, he warned us that following him could possibly lead to our death.

"If anyone serves Me, he must (continue to faithfully) follow Me (without hesitation, holding steadfastly to Me, conforming to My example in living and, if need be, suffering or perhaps dying because of faith in Me) and wherever I am (in heaven's glory), there will My servant be also. If anyone serves Me, the Father will honor him." —John12:26, AMP

If we believe what the Bible plainly declares—that our sovereign God is calling a great multitude of people to be his own—we must also embrace the wonderful, breathtaking privilege to proclaim the hope of Jesus. We must share the gospel with those who don't know him, even if it's not popular. Otherwise, like the Old Testament Israelites, we've abandoned repentance and reverential fear in our Almighty God and replaced it with self-centered disobedience.

Think It Through

- The Israelites blue-tasseled clothing marked them as God-dependent to other nations. How do people around you know that you're God-dependent?

- Do you know a mighty spiritual warrior who is boldly sharing her faith? How does her authentic Christian witness inspire you?

- Do you believe that Jesus is the hope of the world? How do your actions line up with your thoughts?

Chapter 3

Doubt Counts You Out

∞∞∞

"But he did not doubt or waiver in unbelief concerning the promise
of God, but he grew strong and empowered by faith, giving glory to
God, being fully convinced that God had the power to do
what He had promised."

—ROMANS 4:20-21, AMP

∞∞∞

What happens if we don't embrace the blue-cord principles of realizing we serve a living God who expects us to follow his commands and share him with others? Someone else—especially adherents of Islam—will continue to fill the spiritual void. Did you know that Islam is growing at two and a half times the rate of Christianity worldwide, doubling every ten years in America? It's the fastest-growing religion in Canada and Europe.[19] While it's true that the birth rate of Muslims is higher than Christians, Muslims are kingdom-minded, purposeful, and strategic about sharing their faith.

Consider this: while the Catholic church in America has been experiencing big losses of Latinos in its membership, Islam has been strategically working the situation. Harold Morales writes, "The Islamic mandate to propagate the religious teachings to non-Muslims has encouraged many Latino Muslim groups to organize around the production of English and Spanish language books, flyers, and websites directed at Latino audiences."[20]

And as of this writing, the most converts to Islam have been Protestant Christians.[21] Yes, let that soak in for a moment.

Just like we're supposed to be sharing our Christian faith, Dawah, the propagation of Islam, is a religious mandate for Muslims. Here's a quick story to illustrate how Islam expands. My friend Ana had been a follower of Jesus for a few years when I met her. When she first came to America's heartland from an Islamic nation, she didn't know anything about Jesus. She'd never heard about him because telling the gospel in her home country was illegal. All she knew about Christianity was what her mother (and Hollywood) told her: "Be wary of the Christian infidels because they drink, do drugs, and have sex outside marriage." She believed this to be true.

Ana kept her distance. She didn't want an infidel Christian to suck her into degrading immorality, as if Christian immorality was like a cold or flu virus that could be caught. And yet the more time she spent with Christians in her college study group, the more she genuinely liked them. She became deeply concerned about where they'd be spending eternity and believed it was her moral duty to convert them to Islam. So she proactively took classes at her local mosque to learn how to evangelize others. Was she successful? Here's what she says. "Christian students were easy to convert. Their faith was weak, and they didn't really know what they believed." Does that sting your ears as much as it does mine?

A young woman in my focus groups only reinforced this. "I can see how nominal Christian students might convert to Islam. If my faith were not stronger, I might have converted, too. Most of my fellow classmates are Muslim. It's like the United Nations on my university campus. Many women come from Saudi Arabia and other Islamic countries. I've been trying hard to be politically correct and not offend students from other faiths and cultures.

Yet my Muslim friends are bold and wholehearted about sharing their faith. I can't even count how many times they've invited me to their mosques and community events. They're certainly not afraid of offending me."

The Perfect Storm

This is a wake-up call for our generation. If Christianity's decline and Islam's growth continues unchecked, Muslims are projected to outnumber Christians within just a few generations in Europe, Canada, and even here in America. This is a problem. Christians and Muslims alike who live in modern-day Islamic-ruled nations lack religious freedoms and face extreme difficulties. I don't want this kind of life for my children's children. Do you?

Don't misunderstand me. This is not a book about fearing Islam, building walls, or keeping people from other nations out. I only share these things with you to amplify Christianity's declining influence in public life. God is bringing the nations to us, and we're not sharing Jesus. This should leave us face-down on the floor in repentance. When we're not embracing the blue-cord principles in our neighborhoods and workplaces, we're creating a vacuum being filled by those with an Islamic affiliation, or no religious affiliation at all. Can you see the impact this vacuum is creating in our country?

Jesus warned us these things would happen when we lost our Christian influence. "You are the salt of the earth, but if salt has lost its taste, how shall its saltiness be restored? It is no longer good for anything except to be thrown out and trampled under people's feet" (Matthew 5:13, ESV). I don't think any Christian would say, "I don't want to influence anyone for Christ, just throw me out and trample me now." Yet I can't help but think that while we've all been busy doing many churchy things, we might have missed the most important thing—loving God and other people enough to tell them about the good news of Jesus and passing that fervor to the next generation.

Intolerant

It stung my ears when a young, church-going Christian scolded me for being intolerant. I'd challenged her to love women of other faiths and cultures enough to share the good news of Jesus, and it really riled her up. She believed that what I was advocating was "hate speech." She had adopted a cultural belief that every religion is fundamentally the same. She believed that sharing our biblical faith is pushy and insensitive. She wanted to take a part of Jesus and mold him into what she wanted him to be, then add a friendly, happy, Hollywood version of another faith. I realized then that she didn't have a real understanding of who God is, who she was in him, and what he had called her to do. Sadly, no one had passed on to her the blue-cord reminder that she served a living, holy God who called her to be an ambassador for Christ. She'd been raised in the church, and yet she believed a counterfeit lie. How does this happen?

This compelling quote is often attributed to Dwight L. Moody, an American evangelist at the turn of the century: "Out of 100 men, one will read the Bible, the other 99 will read the Christian." I don't know if he ever said it, yet it rings true. Part of Christianity's decline in Westernized nations is that Christians, such as the young woman I mentioned, are "reading" other Christians and not the Bible. This is dangerous and leaves us weak-kneed and vulnerable to lies and deception. I've noticed that many Christians are ill-prepared to share their faith because they don't know who God is, what his Word says, and what he's called us to do. Doubt counts them out.

The only way to identify what's counterfeit is by studying the real thing. I've had many friends of other faiths read the Bible to prove that it had been corrupted only to find that reading it radically transformed their lives. They became wholehearted followers of Jesus with great moral courage who passionately shared their faith despite great persecution. Here's why: God's word is "living and active...piercing to the division of soul and of spirit... discerning the thoughts and intentions of the heart" (Hebrews 4:12, ESV).

King David tells us that when he sought after the Lord and the authority of his Word, God delivered him from fear. And he was inspired to magnify the Lord to those around him (see Psalm 34).

Being rooted in your biblical faith will raise your awareness that you are not wrestling against "flesh and blood but against...cosmic powers over this present darkness, against the spiritual forces of evil in the heavenly places" (Ephesians 4:12, ESV). With this battle waging all around us, the apostle Paul urges us to "take up the whole armor of God" so that we can stand firm, keep alert, and persevere (Ephesians 6:13, ESV). Are you wielding this armor today?

Listen, Satan doesn't want you to realize the full scope of who God is, who you are in him, and what he is calling you to do. Satan wants you to keep wrestling in doubt and unbelief. He wants you to stay busy—away from Bible study and prayer. He wants to keep you in a Christian bubble with Bible verses on your walls and porches, walking with other Christians who don't know the Word, sectioned off together in church. He wants you to believe that all good people are going to heaven, regardless of what we all believe. He wants you to think I'm crazy for suggesting otherwise.

I get it. I was once like the young Christian woman I described and wasn't reading my Bible either. So when it came to sharing my faith, doubt, and unbelief crept in. And that was a dangerous thing.

Only One Way

Once some friends and I went to a neighborhood mosque to observe prayers. I knew very little about Islam, and this field trip was a big step outside my comfort zone. My heart pounded as I shed my shoes, donned a headscarf, and walked up the stairs into the section where women went to pray. Several mothers smiled and greeted me warmly while their small children ran between our feet. When the call to prayer sounded over a loudspeaker, the women gathered quickly, standing side-by-side facing Mecca. I observed them pray in unison—standing, bowing, prostrating low to the ground. Five times they went through this ritual. Peeking through a window, I could see the men below doing the same routine.

As I observed the prayer spoken in Arabic, I didn't know they were reciting in unison, "...all praise belongs to Allah, Lord of all the worlds... You alone do we worship."[22] While they were basically renouncing Christ, I was mesmerized by how pious the women appeared. As I watched them, I thought: "I'm a Christian, and yet my own prayer life is not so earnest." I was filled with shame. I imagined that I didn't have as much zeal for God or prayer as they did.

I shared my thoughts with my friend Salma, herself a former Muslim from a closed Islamic country. She had attended that same mosque when she first came to America. She chided me. "Karen, their prayers are not like your prayers. You pray to the one true, living God! Many of those women you saw were likely going through the motions while thinking about their kids or what they'll cook for dinner. Some feel pressure to be seen as a good Muslim, and that's why they do that ritual prayer. And others are working very hard to please God as they know him."

People have different beliefs about who God is. And I'm thankful to live in a country where people are free to pursue their beliefs. But here's the thing about different beliefs, they can't all be completely true. I love how succinctly David Platt puts it: "God either exists or he doesn't, which makes one person's beliefs true and the other's false, regardless of how passionately one holds that belief."[23] Now more than ever, we must know what God's Word says so that we know what we believe.

Once I got past my personal shame that my prayers were not as earnest as I imagined theirs were, I was struck by the differences between my biblical faith and Islam. I knew in my head that more than a billion Muslims, Hindus, Buddhists, and more in the world don't believe that Jesus is God. Yet the implications were never so real as on that night.

Every single one of the mothers I met was gracious and hospitable. They were good women. And they loved their children dearly and were working hard for them to have a better future. They seemed to be kingdom-minded, working hard to please God as they knew him so they could get to paradise. And yet the differences between us were stark. I believe that Jesus is God. They do not. I believe Jesus died on the cross for my sins. They do not. Either Jesus is the Son of God and the Savior of the world, or he is not. We cannot both be right.

A Counterfeit Reality

After observing the prayer, my friends and I visited with the Imam (the mosque's leader), who patiently answered our questions about Islam. Hearing him amplify the *similarities* between Islam and Christianity was fascinating. A believer in the room that night who didn't know her biblical faith, she might have easily been led to believe that Christianity and Islam are fundamentally the same. It was like that old serpent Satan was in the room hissing a counterfeit reality, "Did God really say...?"

When we left the mosque, several Christians who observed prayers with us remarked, "Wow, if my faith were not quite so strong, I might have been wooed to follow Islam." I wasn't surprised. Islam is strategically playing for the long game of eternity. Of course, the Imam was wise to gloss over differences. To any self-professing Christian who doesn't really know God's Word, it sounds alike.

At a time when we're sensitive to being seen as intolerant, seeker-friendly Muslim websites tout that, unlike Christianity, Islam embraces diversity and inclusion.[24] It doesn't help that Muslim Americans are the most diverse religious group in the United States.[25] Meanwhile, faith-filled Christians are bending over backward to show how tolerant and politically correct we are. When did we forget who God is, what his Word says, or what he called us to do?

Do They Need Jesus?

This question is the elephant in the room: Do women of other faiths and cultures need Jesus? Women in my focus groups were in vehement agreement, "Yes, yes, and yes!" In rapid-fire succession, these faith-filled women shared, "There is *freedom* for women in Christ that does not exist in other faiths!" And "He came to level the playing ground for all of us." "To *not* share that freedom disrespects them." The Bible tells us Jesus is the way, the truth, and the life. He's the only way to the Father. So if we *truly* believe this and live out our lives according to what we believe, then, of course, we want others to know. We would not be loving if we withheld him.

Listen, I believed that women of other faiths and cultures need Jesus too. Then I had a melt-down in the pita aisle and realized I was full of doubt and uncertainty.

Meltdown in the Pita Aisle

My then-future-husband, Renod, took me to an ethnic grocer to search for real pita bread. He grew up in the Middle East and gently pointed out that the pita I bought at my regular grocer wasn't authentic. I was both curious and excited. I didn't know much about Mediterranean food because I grew up on a farm in America's heartland. My mom mostly used just two spices, salt and pepper. This cultural field trip sounded fun.

The grocer was tucked into the heart of a local Arab community not far from home. I'd never realized it was there. When we stepped in the door, it seemed we'd stepped into another world. Fresh almonds were still in their pods. Renod put long, strange-looking fava beans into our cart. A large bin of fresh olives waited to be brined. These were sights and smells I'd never seen at the local grocery where I shopped.

With cart in hand, I maneuvered into the crowd. Everyone was talking passionately all at once. No one was speaking English. And I was having great fun soaking it all in. The canned food labels were in other languages. And the spice aisle was remarkable. It was a great adventure.

I stopped to smell cardamom and pondered purchasing a bag of Turkish coffee when I realized I was alone. Somehow, I had gotten separated from Renod. Crowds pressed in around me, and I calmly peeked into the nearest aisle. He wasn't there.

I retraced my steps. No sign of him.

Anxious, I scanned the produce aisle. Nothing.

I even called his cell, and he didn't answer. Then this happened in a slow-motion split second: I almost collided with a burqa-covered woman in the pita aisle. She quickly looked down and averted her eyes through a peephole in her black head covering. Her husband and children just stared at me.

"I'm sorry."

There was a hush. I then realized that a sea of Muslim, burqa-clad women were staring at me. Was I the only one without a head-covering? I suddenly felt naked wearing just a t-shirt and shorts. Isn't it interesting that this was my fashion choice that day?

In a classic fight-or-flight response, my "reptilian brain" went into overdrive. I thought enough to pray, "Lord, I'm afraid." The Lord responded with this verse, "I did not give you a spirit of fear..." (2 Timothy 1:7, NLT).

"Yes, I know Lord, but..."

"Love them as I love them," the Lord whispered.

Love! In that moment, I couldn't even say hello. I was afraid of them.

Now I find it interesting that I feared them more than I feared the Lord. David struggled with this fear, too. In Psalm 34, while fearing Abimelech, he acted crazy and learned that "the angel of the LORD encamps around those who fear Him (with awe-inspired reverence and worship Him with obedience). He rescues (each of) them....for those who fear Him there is no want..." (Psalm 34:7, 9 AMP).

I wanted to engage those women as an authentic Christian witness rather than run away from them in fear. I wanted to fully realize God's heart for the lost and embrace my role as an ambassador for Christ. Like the Israelites, I needed to hold onto the blue-cord reminder that God is holy. And he'll help me follow after His way rather than my way.

Something Different about You

Are there places where your spirit senses darkness, where you can almost feel the spiritual forces of evil pressing in? When was the last time you wrestled with the absence of the Lord? The first time I entered my friend Miriam's city, I sensed such darkness, and it filled me with terror. I went into that city naïve, wrestling with unacknowledged doubt and unbelief. I had marshmallow faith. And I vowed never to return again with such small trust in the Lord. Years later when I finally did return, I still felt the Lord's absence. Yet this time, the Light within me was greater than the darkness in the world, and I was unafraid. I'd come "suited up" with the whole armor of God, and the Holy Spirit was shining brightly through me. It happened because I'd begun to seek the Lord with all my heart and spend purposeful time in his Word.

I couldn't believe the transformation. One day while I was there, I prayed with an elderly Syrian refugee who bore a *deq*, a facial tattoo, on her forehead. The fading blue tattoo peaked out from under her hijab, and it connected her with an Arab or Kurd tribal group from long ago. Had I met her years ago, that *deq* peeking out from under her hijab would have intimidated me. I don't think I would have spoken with her. This time I couldn't wait to tell her about Jesus, and I felt only love. My husband had just preached a sermon from John 7:38 that "whoever believes in me...out of his heart will flow rivers of living water" (ESV). This elderly woman clutched my hand and told me through an interpreter that she wanted me to pray that she would have this living water. I was filled with awe over her hunger for the Lord.

Then I noticed another young, hijab-clad woman watching us. Turns out she wanted to pray that same prayer. As we spoke, her eyes misted over with tears. She said something I'll never forget. "I feel something different about you and this place. I don't feel this way at my home. I want this feeling—this light—with me always." Oh my goodness, yes, of course I could tell her about the source of that Light.

"The light shines in the darkness, and the darkness has not overcome it" (John 1:5, ESV). Oh, I wish you could have experienced that holy moment with me. She accepted Jesus as her Lord and Savior, then she went on to tell her sister about the Light shining into the darkness.

What if I had not been rooted in God's word and still been wrestling with unbelief and doubt on that trip? What if I'd forgotten I served a holy God and been consumed with not wanting to offend that elderly woman? What if I didn't have the moral courage to tell that young woman how she could have the light of Jesus with her forever? How many other times have I held back from sharing Jesus with those who desperately needed him because I feared people more than I feared the Lord? How many times have you held back as well?

The Battle Is Already Won

What if you knew that immigrants, international students, and refugees here might already assume you're a Christian? How would your actions change if you knew they might even be disappointed if you were hiding your Christian faith? What if sharing your faith with them isn't actually as hard as you've imagined?

What if you could grab hold of the blue-cord principles to quiet any unbelief or doubt in your ability to share Jesus? What if you could push back against modern-day resistance and change someone's life for eternity?

Could you do that?

Of course in your own power, you couldn't do any of these things. "With people (as far as it depends on them) it is impossible, but with God all things are possible" (Matthew 19:26, AMP).

All things are possible with God. Does this encourage you as much as it does me?

Let me encourage you some more. Did you know that God has been using everyday women just like you and me for over two thousand years to make major contributions to the spread of Christianity? Since antiquity, through seemingly impossible obstacles, such as life-threatening persecution and horrific pandemics, mothers, sisters, and friends have locked arms and leaned in to share the hope of Jesus in their generation.[26]

And here's the thing: their contributions weren't isolated or insignificant. In fact, in every era, women's contributions have been immeasurable. (I can't wait to tell you more about that later.) For now, just know a great cloud of faith-filled women witnesses have gone before us and expanded the Kingdom. Most didn't move across the world. They started small right where they lived. And now it's your turn.

You are central to God's story *right now*.

He loves you and values you as his daughter. And he's calling you to declare his glory among the nations *right where you live*. Will you say "yes?"

All God's daughters must make a choice.

While a great spiritual battle is waging for souls all around us, will you succumb to culture and hide that you're a Jesus-follower? Or will you lock arms with me and other blue-cord ambassadors all over the world to shine a Light into the darkness?

My heartfelt prayer is that you won't succumb to the world. No, instead, take this journey with me. Remember, all things are possible with God. Come and see how simple it can be to live as an authentic Christian witness among women of other faiths and cultures. Discover the joy that comes from seeking and trusting God, then declaring his glory. Learning and practicing these blue-cord principles made me brave, strong, and courageous. And I know they'll do the same for you.

Think It Through

- How does doubt or unbelief impact your Christian witness?
- What does it mean to "fear the Lord?" How might a strong fear of the Lord give you the moral courage to share your faith?
- Is Bible study growing your faith as much as you'd like it to? Why or why not?

Chapter 4

Assumptions

◇◇

"And it shall come to pass that everyone who calls on the name
of the Lord shall be saved."

— JOEL 2:32, ESV

◇◇

There are no shortcuts for eradicating doubt and unbelief. Once I realized that Jesus' great commission mandate was for ordinary Christians like me, I had a choice to make. I could slip back into my safe, comfortable, Christian, suburban bubble and pretend I was still exempt. Or I would have to embrace the blue-cord principles of who he is, who I am in him, and that he called me to be a witness in my generation. The first step required putting to rest some erroneous assumptions I'd made about women of other faiths and cultures. I invite you to consider any assumptions you might be harboring as well.

Assuming the Worst

My coworkers and I were in a high-rise building in Dallas when Islamic extremists brought down the Twin Towers in New York City on September

11, 2001. I'll never forget the panicky uncertainty my coworkers and I felt as we fled down twenty-two flights of stairs together. At the bottom, we all huddled in the building's small café, watching in horror as a second plane ripped through another tower. Everyone alive back then has a story like this from that day, when the world began growing smaller and larger at the same time.

Before that day, I hadn't given Muslims any thought. From then on, I noticed them everywhere. It's a wonder that I'd never seen them before. Given the circumstances, it's not surprising that I initially feared them. If you were alive then, you probably did too. It took years for me to realize that when Jesus said, "Go into all the world and proclaim the gospel to the whole creation," he didn't add, "except for Muslims" (Mark 16:15, ESV).

The Lord had radically transformed my heart for Muslims by the time my husband and I founded a non-profit ministry, iHOPE Ministries. We set out to inspire and empower everyday Christians to share the hope of Jesus with Muslims and other non-believers. At the time, the large metroplex where we lived had just seventeen mosques. (Now there are over eighty.) Back then, we naively believed that Christians would enthusiastically embrace the need to reach Muslims and people of other faiths and cultures in our city with the gospel. We were wrong. We quickly discovered that most Christians weren't interested in sharing their faith with people of other faiths and cultures.

Undeterred and full of faith, we rented a room from our neighborhood community center and promoted the first iHOPE Ministries workshop with everyone in our circle of influence. We set out to empower at least twenty-five everyday believers to share Jesus with Muslims. When more than one hundred people from all over the city registered, we were shocked. Scrambling, we borrowed lawn chairs from everyone we knew, and still, the workshop was standing room only. Teachers, medical professionals, students, real estate agents—men, women, and teens—had all witnessed the influx of people of other faiths and cultures coming into their neighborhoods. And all of them wondered how to live as authentic Christian witnesses among them. "I know I should be sharing my faith with my Muslim (neighbor, coworker, classmate). I came here to learn how." Through grassroots word-of-mouth, iHOPE trained more than 7,500 Christians in the first five years. As those believers began putting into action what they learned, they began sharing their faith with everyone, not just Muslims.

Through those early years, we tested various marketing messages to promote workshops. We discovered that just a smattering of seminary students and those preparing for long-term missions would attend the "Come learn to love your Muslim neighbors" workshop. In contrast, this more shocking workshop title would draw hundreds: "Come learn about our Islamic problem." The content was always the same: five essentials every Christian should know and do with Muslims and other non-believers. Interestingly, the most unloving title would always draw the largest crowd.

Most of the people hadn't yet interacted with people of other faiths and cultures. They were looking for ways to protect themselves. Shirin Taber, creator of *"Live What You Believe,"* a human rights and religious-freedom training online, shares that "Interacting with people different from us can lead us to want to protect ourselves. Sometimes it's a fear of loss of identity or that our community might change."[27]

The faith-filled women in my focus groups echoed these thoughts. "So many Christian women in my circles have their heart in politics right now. It's getting in the way of sharing our faith," Lydia reflected. "I've tried hanging out with some of my new Hindu and Buddhist neighbors to live as an authentic Christian witness. Yet the women in my Christian community shame me as if I'm betraying my own biblical beliefs. They're uncomfortable with me engaging with people who aren't like them."

"I live in a very conservative area," said Sarah. "Twenty miles away, there's an extremely liberal town, and many of my conservative Christian friends say they'd never go there. They stay as far away as possible because they just don't know how to interact with the people who live there. When you've lived your life in the bubble and haven't traveled or had friends of other faiths, it can be really scary. We don't know how to approach people who look or act different or who practice a different faith."

Jen shares, "My local discount store has a check-out attendant who wears a head covering. I've seen believers step out of her aisle once they realize she's checking them out. When I see it, I think, *Wow. It has been decades since 9/11*. It reminds me of my mother, who harbored discriminating thoughts against the Japanese for decades after World War II."

Assumptions

Have you noticed Christians self-segregating, assuming the worst of people of other faiths and cultures? Have you done it as well? I surely did. Before I was seriously determined to share my faith with women who were different from me, I had to put to rest all the assumptions I'd been making about women of other faiths and cultures. Have you carried any of these misperceptions?

That they...

- Already know all about Jesus
- Wouldn't be interested in hearing what Christians believe
- Wouldn't want to give up everything to follow Jesus
- Would be offended if I started a spiritual conversation
- Want to keep to themselves
- Might be terrorists
- Other misperceptions

Our teenage son made a costly assumption that he could drive with the check-engine light on indefinitely and learned an old saying: "You know what happens when you assume? It makes an 'ass' out of u and me." Once I realized that I'd been an ass, making assumptions about women of other faiths and cultures, I knew I needed to step out of my introverted comfort zone. Only then did I discover so many women of other faiths and cultures who are desperately seeking Jesus. How will they believe in him if we don't tell them (see Romans 10:14)?

Albania to America

Esther's story grips my heart and captures my imagination because her home country is a great case study for what can happen when a nation's believers don't share and instead succumb to secularism.

In the summer of 1990 in Albania, Esther was in the eighth grade. Her country had just become a democratic nation, and missionaries flooded in to spread the word of God. "One day, some Jehovah's Witnesses knocked on our door and asked me if I wanted to be saved. I asked them what 'being saved' meant. They told me about God, Jehovah, and Jesus Christ, then gave me a Bible and several magazines to read," Esther recounts. "I really wanted to believe God, yet I was so confused and perplexed with all the different religions and all the different pathways to heaven."

Esther grew up in a Muslim family in Albania, a tiny country in southeastern Europe that had been under communist rule for forty-five years. In medieval times, Albania was mostly Christian. Then Arabs raided the country in the late ninth century, prompting a rise in Islam. Eventually, Islam became Albania's majority religion throughout centuries of Ottoman rule. By the mid-1940s, a communist regime came into power. And in 1967, the country declared itself the world's first atheist state. All forms of religious practice were banned. The nation of Albania was in turmoil, and its people faced religious persecution. Yet many people continued to practice their mostly Islamic faith.

This is what Esther's world was like when the Jehovah's Witnesses knocked on her door. She'd been born into a secular Muslim family in an isolated country that had suffered under decades of communism and religious persecution. It was no wonder she was confused.

That fall, Esther attended an all-girls boarding school in the capital city of Tirana, a few hours from her hometown. The school was operated by a Turkish Muslim company that claimed an academic focus. Yet during her four-year tenure there, she experienced the school was really focused on spreading Islam.

"While I was at that boarding school, I met a sweet Christian friend who asked me if I knew God. She smirked when I confided to her that I thought of myself as a Jehovah's Witness," Esther confides. "She urged me to read the Bible carefully. Then she told me that God would reveal himself to me." In that Turkish Muslim school, Esther read a Bible in secret, mostly to prove to her friend that she was wrong about Jehovah's Witnesses. "With so much love, hunger, and thirst for God, I felt I was on the right path. I wanted to prove to my friend that being a Jehovah's Witness was the right path to God." While reading the Bible, Esther fell in love with the Word, and the Lord Jesus met her right where she was.

"It was just the two of us, Jesus and me—no outside influence. As I studied God's Word, I gave my life to our precious Savior, the Lord Jesus Christ. I was very hungry to grow in my faith and fellowship with other believers," says Esther. "The Lord was working on my heart daily, yet I couldn't go to church on the weekends because I was on a Muslim campus and the school didn't allow it. I wanted to be baptized immediately when I read the passages of baptism in the Bible. I urgently wanted to follow all the Lord's commands."

Privilege

Christianity has long been a large part of America's social fabric. In Canada's formative years, the prevailing views on morality were largely based on the Bible. Europe was the birthplace of the Protestant reformation. You and I are free to read our Bibles without persecution. We can worship and share our faith with anyone we like. We can freely choose to follow Jesus (or not) without compulsion. And according to Pew Research, despite the declining number of self-professing Christians, there are still more Jesus-followers in America than any other nation.[28]

The Israelites enjoyed great privileges too, back when the Lord provided the symbolic blue cord. They could visibly see God's divine presence always surrounding them with a cloud pillar (see 1 Corinthians 10:1). They experienced God's miraculous intervention first-hand when he parted the Red Sea (see Exodus 14:29). Their spiritual leader, Moses, even spoke directly with God. With so many touchpoints of God's presence and privilege, you'd think they would be walking closely with him. Yet they weren't. God wasn't pleased with many of them. He scattered them in the wilderness because they waivered in doubt and disobedience (see Numbers 14:29). Paul tells us, "These things happened to them as an example and warning (to us); they were written for our instruction (to admonish and equip us), upon whom the ends of the ages have come" (1 Corinthians 1:11, AMP).

Let's take this warning to heart. We're living in the "end of the ages." And it's no accident that you and I are on earth in this generation. If we keep wrestling with assumptions that keep us from sharing our faith, our country could easily go the way of Albania.

Everyday Ordinary Witness

"With the rise of globalization and polarizing trends in our world, there are many new threats. We have many new choices to make and more questions than answers. And yet there are also new opportunities," shares Shirin Taber in *Empowering Women Media.*[29] Never before have ordinary Christians had the opportunity to befriend and share the gospel with so many women from previously hard-to-reach places. We have much work to do.

What would it look like if all the Christian women like you and I embraced the blue-cord principles and began to share our faith, in love, with neighbors who didn't act, look, or think like we do?

The story you're about to read is especially dear to me because Kim never imagined sharing her faith with women of other faiths. She'd rarely encounter people who were not already believers. When a serious family health crisis hit, no one would have blamed her if she had been too anxious or too busy to notice two women of other faiths who didn't know Jesus in her midst. To be tolerant and inoffensive, she could have held back and kept the good news to herself. She could have assumed that they already knew about Jesus and wouldn't want to hear. Yet in doing any of these things, she would have missed out on the privilege of sharing Jesus and on the holy, joyful, awe-inspiring moment that one of them became a daughter of the King.

Kim's Story

At the start of the COVID-19 pandemic, Kim's eighty-two-year-old mother suffered a near-fatal heart attack. In anticipation of her mother's release from the hospital, Kim pulled a team of caregivers together to aid in her recovery. She never imagined that the first person to arrive would be Farrah, a Muslim immigrant from Nigeria. Soon after, another caregiver from another faith arrived. "My family was in crisis, and the Lord sent two women from other faiths and cultures to rally together toward a common purpose to help my mom thrive," Kim recounts.

While the two women cared for her mom, Kim looked for opportunities to get to know them. One day, Kim noticed that Farrah frequently told her mother to "have faith." Curious, Kim asked her, "What does faith mean to you?" As she listened, she realized that Farrah's view of faith was very different from her own biblical view. Asking that one simple question prompted rich, ongoing discussions about God and who Christians believed he was. It was a blue-cord moment for Kim to remember she served a living, holy God and that she was his witness.

The bond between them grew as they continued to get to know one another. Farrah would ask Kim and her mother questions about their lives, and they had great fun sharing. By now, the three women trusted one other, and Kim asked, "What's your story?" Farrah shared her life's story, full of loss and hurts. Kim and her mother listened with compassion and love. That day, when it was time for her to go, Farrah lingered at the door. "Will you pray for me?" she whispered as she gathered her personal belongings to leave.

Kim wouldn't let her slip out that easily. "May I pray with you right now, in Jesus' name?" Farrah nodded, and they stood there together, new friends, socially distanced in her kitchen. Kim closed her eyes and bowed her head. She paused to still her heart and seek the Lord about what to pray for Farrah. After "in Jesus's name, Amen," Kim opened her eyes to see Farrah visibly touched.

In the middle of a pandemic and a family crisis, God used Kim to point both Farrah and another caregiver to Jesus in ways she never imagined. Every day she sought the Lord for wisdom to see what the Father was doing and to know what she should do. And she discovered that the Holy Spirit always guided her.

One day, as Easter was drawing near, Kim asked Farrah what she knew about Easter. Farrah replied, "Doesn't it have something to do with eggs?" That opened the door for Kim to share the Gospel of Jesus Christ. Afterward, Farrah said, "Thank you for sharing this with me. I really appreciate knowing the truth." In the days leading up to Easter, Kim and Farrah had several rich conversations about what Christians believed.

Then on Good Friday, Kim walked into the room as her mother and Farrah watched a pastor on television leading an invitation to accept Christ. Kim felt the Holy Spirit's presence in the room and just knew "she's praying that prayer." After the invitation, Kim asked, "Farrah, did you pray that prayer?"

"Yes," she said.

Oh, the privilege of leading someone to Christ! Kim danced around the room as Farrah beamed with tears of joy, celebrating the moment Farrah became a daughter of the King. I like to imagine all the angels in heaven dancing as well.

A Blue-Cord Moment

If you're thinking to yourself, "I could never do that," think again. Remember when I told you that I grew up on a farm in the Midwest and never knew women of other faiths and cultures? Well into adulthood, I believed that sharing the gospel was only for super-Christian missionaries overseas. I was largely apathetic about taking an active role in the great commission. Then God transformed me through the blue-cord principles. One day, I found myself sharing Jesus for the first time, in the most remarkable way. I pray this story encourages and challenges you.

On a long ride home from the airport after an international flight, my Uber driver asked me where I'd been. I was bleary-eyed and grouchy and didn't feel much like talking. I told him I'd just come in from the Middle East, thinking that would appease him. But I saw the opposite happen. He was from Pakistan, and from the clues I could see in his car, I thought he might be Muslim. In polite chit-chat, I casually mentioned I was a follower of Jesus.

"I'm Muslim. I don't know much about Jesus. Can you tell me about him?" he asked.

Yes, you read that right. He wanted to know more.

Years before, I had sat in the backseat of a taxi just like this. Back then, I was in Beirut with my friend Caroline. She'd asked her Muslim driver if he knew Jesus, which started a rich conversation about what Christians believed. I couldn't even imagine having such a conversation in America. Yet here I was, on the cusp of sharing Jesus with my Pakistani Muslim Uber driver. This was a blue-cord moment, a time to remember that I serve a living, holy God and that he put me here in this taxi to share the good news of Jesus Christ. So I shared what it means to be a Christian, all the while praying in my heart that I wouldn't mess it up (as if everything depended on me).

"I believe what God says in the Holy Bible in Romans 10:9, that if you confess with your mouth that Jesus is Lord and believe in your heart that God raised him from the dead, you'll be saved."

"How do you know that is the truth?" he asked.

"Well, if you are open to it, I could pray with you that God's Holy Spirit would reveal the truth to you about Jesus."

He became very quiet and stopped asking questions. And I began to second-guess myself. Did I share it right? What could I have said differently? When he pulled up into my driveway, he shocked me.

"Would you pray that prayer for me now?"

We prayed together, my Pakistani Muslim Uber driver and me. I wish you could have been there to see it. We stood in my cul-de-sac right next to his little blue car, trunk popped, luggage in hand, while my atheist neighbors watched on. It was surreal. We bowed our heads and prayed together that God's Holy Spirit would reveal the truth to him about Jesus. That day, light cut through the darkness. It was the first time I'd shared my faith in America.

Where the spirit of the Lord is, there is freedom (see 2 Corinthians 3:17). Why had I been so afraid to share my faith before? Why had I made so many assumptions? Living out the blue-cord principles transformed my life. Since then, I've seen them transform many other people as well. Let's get you started on this journey.

Think It Through

- What assumptions have you made about women of other faiths and cultures?

- The rise of globalization and polarization brings new threats and opportunities. What opportunities do you see for everyday Christians?

- Can you imagine yourself leading a woman of another faith or culture to Christ? Why or why not?

Chapter 5

The Most Important Need

◇◇◇

"Anyone who is not with me is against me,
and anyone who does not gather with me scatters."

–LUKE 11:23, CSB

◇◇◇

Can you imagine yourself leading a woman from another faith or culture to Christ? Are you willing to put yourself out there and practice doing it?

If you're still reading, I'm guessing your answer is "yes." These are important questions for you and other faith-filled women to wrestle with because being apathetic or neutral about sharing your faith is not a viable option for Jesus-followers. Jesus warns us that "anyone who does not gather with Me scatters" (Luke 11:23, CSB). This is a hard line. If you're not in the business of gathering, then you're scattering and working in opposition to our Savior. Jesus forces us all to make a choice about taking an active role in being his witnesses. We are either in or we're out. There is no in-between. We are all called to be making the most of our time on earth, recognizing and taking advantage of every opportunity to point people to him (see Ephesians 5:16).

Over the last decade, my husband and I have inspired and empowered tens of thousands of Christians to share the hope of Jesus with people of other faiths and cultures. Most knew they should be sharing, yet many obstacles were in the way. One of the biggest? A lack of compassion. There's always a pivotal moment when the Lord gives us the compassion that compels us to share our faith. This moment happened to Connie in the twinkling of an eye.

"I could only see her dark, soulful eyes, and slowly, slowly, she started to take off her burqa. And then I could see that there was a real woman underneath that black cloak. And it was so disarming because she was a stunningly beautiful woman standing there in front of me. And as she told me her heart-breaking coming-to-Jesus story, I realized that she had feelings and emotions. And that she had hungered for the hope and peace that only Jesus could bring. It was such a powerful moment. I'll never forget it. It gave me compassion for women of other faiths and cultures and prompted me to take an active role in the great commission."

Once filled with compassion, Connie began sharing her faith with women of other faiths and cultures worldwide. Now she is taking other women by the hand to do the same.

How about you? Have you experienced a moment like this—a time when you've realized in your core that women of other faiths and cultures are perishing without the hope of Jesus? And has this "knowing" amplified your compassion to take action, to share your faith? If that hasn't been your experience, keep reading. You are sure to be encouraged by this story.

More than one hundred women of other faiths and cultures first heard about Jesus from Jackie. She's led dozens to Christ. Yet when she first set out to share her faith, she didn't feel any compassion, which kept her from taking action.

"I've been a believer since I was eight. I was raised in church and grew up knowing I should share the Gospel. But the truth is, I didn't, at least not in an intentional way. I carried around a lot of fear and perceived obstacles—things that prevented me from sharing. I knew they were all excuses. I began earnestly praying that I would be someone who shares her faith. In a few months, God put on my heart the compassion I needed to share Jesus with women of other faiths and cultures. Compassion moved me into action."

You Can't Fake This

Compassion will move you into action. And guess what, you can't fake it. You either have it or you don't. When I first set out to share my faith with women of other faiths and cultures, I didn't have it. Connie and Jackie didn't have it. You might not have it either. Yet it's important to have because Jesus modeled compassion for us, and we're supposed to copy him. Jesus always had a compassionate response to the needs of the people around him. Take a look:

"When He (Jesus) saw the crowds, he had compassion for them, because they were harassed and helpless, like a sheep without a shepherd" (Matthew 9:36, ESV).

"When he (Jesus) went ashore, he saw a great crowd, and he had compassion on them and healed their sick" (Matthew 14:14, ESV).

"And a leper came to Him, begging Him... Moved with compassion, Jesus reached out with His hand and touched him..." (Mark 1:40-41, AMP).

Jesus had compassion for the hemorrhaging woman, too. Read again what happened when this faith-filled woman touched the blue-corded tassels on Jesus' garment. Notice Jesus' compassionate response.

"Then a woman who had suffered from a hemorrhage for twelve years came up and touched the (tassel) fringe of His outer robe; for she had been saying to herself, 'If I only touch His outer robe, I will be healed.' But Jesus, turning and seeing her said, 'Take courage daughter, your (personal trust and confident) faith (in Me) has made you well.' And at once the woman was (completely) healed" (Matthew 9:20-22, AMP).

People quickly learned that Jesus healed the hemorrhaging woman, and news spread. In the New Testament, Matthew records a moment when Jesus' compassionate miracle moved a whole group of people to compassion.

And when the men of that place recognized Him (Jesus), they sent word throughout all the surrounding district and brought to Him all who were sick; and they begged Him to let them merely touch the fringe of his robe, and all who touched it were perfectly restored" (Matthew 14:35-36, AMP).

Imagine being so moved with compassion for the women around you who don't know Jesus that you become compelled to take action, to bring those women to Jesus. When you put on compassion, the Lord will give you what you need to cross-cultural and religious divides to bring women to Jesus too.

Compassion Compels Action

How do you get compassion? Start by grasping the blue-cord principle that you are one of God's chosen people. You are holy, well-loved, and set apart for God's purpose. Then you pray for and "put on" compassion, praying and yearning for it to spring out from your heart and into action (see Colossians 3:12). Paul tells us to "Put on then, as God's chosen ones, holy and beloved, compassionate hearts..." (Colossians 3:12, ESV).

Compassion will bubble up from your empathy. When you empathize, you recognize someone's need for Jesus and imagine how you might feel if you were that person, lost without the hope and peace that only Jesus can bring. Practicing empathy alone won't compel you to action. When you practice compassion, you take it further. Practicing compassion will compel you to action. When you put on compassion, you will feel compelled to bring people to Jesus, just like the men who brought people to touch Jesus' blue-tasseled hem for healing,

Don't mistake empathy for compassion. Having empathy is a good first step. Yet practicing compassion will propel you to action. Faith-filled women can empathize and build relationships for years on everything but Jesus. And a blue-cord, compassionate woman will take action—no matter how small—to intentionally point a non-believer to Christ.

What if you don't have as much compassion as you'd like? I say, "Relax and trust God." You can cultivate and grow compassion. Here's a story in Genesis that illustrates a time when Joseph's compassion grew.

> "He (Joseph) lifted up his eyes and saw his brother Benjamin, his mother's son, and said, 'Is this your youngest brother...?' Then Joseph hurried out, for his compassion grew warm for his brother, and he sought a place to weep (Genesis 43:29-30, ESV).

Compassion caused Joseph to weep, to be vulnerable, to be fully human. describes compassion like this,

"Compassion asks us to go where it hurts, to enter into the places of pain, to share in brokenness, fear, confusion, and anguish. Compassion challenges us to cry out with those in misery, to mourn with those who are lonely, to weep with those in tears. Compassion requires us to be weak with the weak, vulnerable with the vulnerable, and powerless with the powerless. Compassion means full immersion in the condition of being human."[30]

It's life on life, my friend. I pray that every faith-filled woman would cultivate this kind of compassion—the kind that causes us to weep for those who are lost and fall face down in repentance because we haven't been intentionally sharing Jesus with those who so desperately need his peace. If you genuinely seek more compassion from the Lord, he will hear you and give you what you need (see John 14:13-14).

Go and Do Likewise

How does practicing compassion look in real life? Let's say you cultivated a relationship with your new Hindu neighbor and discovered she's wrestling with serious marriage problems. You empathize with her struggles and try to imagine what it must be like to live without Jesus during such a hard time. You might say,

"I'm so sorry to hear about what you're going through right now. I can only imagine how hard this must be for you. How can I be praying for you?"

This is relational empathy, and it's a good first step. An offer to pray for a woman of another faith or culture is always a good thing. And yet it's passive. When you practice compassion, you take your empathy to the next level by "bringing" your friend to Jesus. Remember, compassion will compel you to action. Here's how to take that next step:

"I'm so sorry to hear about what you're going through. I can only imagine how hard this must be for you. *You know I'm a follower of Jesus, and I believe what the Holy Bible tells us in Romans (8:34 ESV) that Jesus 'is at the right hand of God" and "is interceding for us. Would you allow me to pray to God with you now, in the name of Jesus?"*

By taking an intentional next step, inviting a friend of another faith to pray *with* you in Jesus' name, you practice compassion through action.

Compassion Crosses Cultural Boundaries

In addition to modeling compassion, Jesus told stories that illustrate compassion in action. Jesus' parable of the Good Samaritan illustrates that your compassion should cross cultural and religious boundaries.

Here's an overview: A Jewish man was robbed, beaten, and left for dead. Both a priest and a Levite—two religious people you would think most likely to help—saw the hurting man and walked on by. They did nothing. Then a Samaritan, an un-named man from a hated race synonymous with a heretic, saw the Jew in the road. His reaction was starkly different.

But a Samaritan, as he journeyed, came to where he was, and *when he saw him, he had compassion.* He went to him and bound up his wounds, pouring on oil and wine. Then he set him on his own animal and brought him to an inn and took care of him. And the next day he took out two denarii and gave them to the innkeeper, saying, "Take care of him, and whatever more you spend, I will repay you when I come back." —Luke 10:33-35, ESV

When he saw him, compassion immediately swelled within him and compelled him to action. Compassion sliced through deep, divisive, hate-filled cultural and religious divides.

After sharing this story, Jesus asked a young lawyer, "Which of these three (the priest, the Levite, or the Samaritan) do you think proved to be a neighbor to the man who fell among the robbers?" The young lawyer responded, "The one who showed him mercy." And Jesus said to him, "You go and do likewise" (Luke 10:36-37, ESV).

Katie's Story

Katie spent a lifetime allowing many things to get in the way of sharing her faith. As a corporate executive, it was hard for her to admit that she'd been "scattering" instead of "gathering." Katie confides, "The problem was that I didn't feel much compassion for the lost, especially women of other faiths and cultures. Something needed to change."

Katie started small by grasping the blue-cord principles. She prayed that the Lord would remind her daily that she is holy, well-loved, and set apart for his purposes. Then she prayed that the Lord would replace her apathy for the lost with compassion. With a softened heart, she soon began taking baby steps across cultural and religious boundaries as an ambassador for Christ. She couldn't believe it when she began feeling green shoots of fresh compassion and began leading women of other faiths and cultures to Christ. She no longer viewed ordinary, everyday events as coincidental. She realized that her mission field is the space between herself and the person next to her who doesn't know Jesus. Here's one of Katie's stories. May it inspire you to begin your own journey as a compassionate ambassador for Christ.

Katie was involved in community development, and the first thing she noticed about Rani was her passionate work for the poor and marginalized within a nearby Muslim Sudanese community. After fleeing war in the Sudan twenty years prior, Rani had become a successful business owner while raising sons as a single mom. She had grown to become an influential community leader, and her sons copied their mom by pursuing careers in public service. Katie respected and admired Rani's work as a community leader, and as their paths intersected, a friendship was born.

In time, Rani began to confide in Katie about some of the difficult struggles she was facing with some men in the Sudanese community. The men were jealous of Rani's growing influence as a community leader, and they were working hard at undermining her efforts. She suspected it was because she was female. Rani didn't know how to handle the situation.

Katie empathized with Rani's plight because she'd experienced similar leadership challenges in her career. For a time, she just listened as Rani vented. Katie knew in her heart that Rani needed wisdom and understanding from the Almighty living God, a kind of wisdom that she couldn't get from the god of Islam. Yet she couldn't bring herself to take that next step. Frankly, Katie was intimidated. Rani was very influential and involved in her Muslim community. She frequently quoted the Quran. She appeared quite devout.

Katie was stuck and just couldn't bring herself to take that next step. She was considering not saying anything, yet the Holy Spirit had been nudging her. As she talked through the situation with me, I asked, "What's holding you back from pointing her to Jesus?" She bit her lip thoughtfully, "I'm afraid she'll think me pushy if I bring up Jesus."

"Does she know you're a follower of Jesus?"

"Oh, I'm sure she does."

"What did she say when you told her you were a follower of Jesus?"

"Oh, I haven't actually told her. I guess I'm just assuming she knows."

"How is this helping you share the hope of Jesus?" I asked.

"It's not."

"What do you want to do about it?"

Katie had long been sensing the Holy Spirit prompting her to invite Rani to study what the Bible says about leadership and women. Katie's compassion for Rani's situation had been welling up inside of her. Yet she squashed the thought of taking the next step every single time because she feared what Rani might think more than she feared the Lord's mandate to "be his witness" in this area.

Katie had been "scattering," not "gathering." She'd been abdicating her role as an ambassador for Christ. Once she realized this, Katie was heartbroken and compelled to take the next step. She decided she would invite Rani to study the Bible with her.

Now she faced a new hurdle; she didn't know what words she might say.

This is a normal hurdle, yet not insurmountable. I invited her to write down and practice with a friend how she might invite Rani to study the Bible. She didn't need perfect words. She just needed to tell Rani that she was a Jesus-follower, point Rani to Jesus, and invite her to do the study—like she would invite a friend to the movies. Here's where she landed:

> "Rani, I've been thinking about some of the leadership challenges you've shared with me. You know I've had challenges like it in my career, too. There's something that's helped me a lot in this area, and I've not mentioned it yet. You may have guessed that I'm a follower of Jesus. I've found great wisdom and understanding about leadership from the Bible. Would you like to study what the Bible says about leadership with me?"

We prayed that the Lord would remind Katie who she was in him and give her the compassion and courage to follow through. She decided to invite Rani to study the Bible the next time they spoke.

A few days later, Katie called with overwhelming excitement, "Rani said yes! She wants to study the Bible with me starting next Tuesday! And she asked if she could bring some friends along!"

We were overjoyed. Since Katie's compassionate invitation, she's had many deep, rich conversations with Rani about what the Bible says about leadership, women, and the good news of Jesus. Rani has been seeking out Katie to pray with her (in Jesus' name) for her work situation. As of this writing, we're still praying that Rani would become a follower of Jesus.

It's sobering to consider that Rani has lived and worked in America for more than twenty years. Until she met Katie, she didn't know what Christians believed. Katie is the first Christian who ever invited Rani to study the Bible. Katie is the first believer to pray with her in Jesus' name. Through Katie, Rani heard the good news about salvation in Jesus for the very first time. If Katie hadn't pressed through her own fear and personal discomfort to practice compassion, Rani might never have known the truth about Jesus. Many women of other faiths and cultures are likely living near you who will perish because no one has told them the truth about Jesus. But God is not far from them because you live nearby.

Take a Small Step

Friend, when you're filled with compassion for women of other faiths who don't know Jesus, you'll push beyond excuses. You won't merely empathize. When you seek the Lord's heart for the lost and pray wholeheartedly for compassion, the Holy Spirit will compel you to action. And as you begin to practice compassion, you'll take baby steps at crossing cultural and religious boundaries as an ambassador for Christ. Soon you will be reconciling people to God, and you won't view ordinary events as coincidental. In time, you'll come to realize that your mission field is the space between you and the person next to you who doesn't know Jesus.

It all starts with a first step. Grasp the blue-cord principles. Pray that the Lord would remind you that you are holy, well-loved, and set apart for his purposes. Then pray that the Lord would flood your heart with compassion for the lost.

Heavenly Father, you tell us that anyone who does not gather with you scatters. Oh Lord, forgive me for not gathering more people to you. Lord, open the eyes of my heart to realize that I am holy, well-loved, and set apart for your purposes. Flood my heart with compassion for women around me who don't know you. Give me eyes to see women of other faiths and cultures as you see them. Break my heart for them, Lord, and use me to proclaim the good news to them. Amen

Think It Through

- Jesus warns us that "anyone who does not gather with me scatters." Have you been "gathering" or "scattering?" What do you want to be doing going forward?

- Share a moment when you felt such overwhelming compassion for the lost that you were compelled to take action.

- Compassion compels action and crosses cultural and religious divides. What do you need to do to gain more compassion for women of other faiths and cultures?

Chapter 6

Chasing Glory

◇◇

"The heavens declare the glory of God,
and the sky above proclaims his handiwork."

— PSALM 19:1, ESV

◇◇

It feels amazing to get praise and honor from others, doesn't it? Yet the praise of people is shallow and short-lived. If you're like most of the faith-filled women I know, you already believe that you should be seeking God's glory instead of seeking glory for yourself or someone else.

And yet, if you hold back from sharing the good news of Jesus because you're worried about what others might think, you're giving people more glory than God. I'm certainly not telling you something you don't already know. Most of the Christian women in my focus groups struggled with this same issue.

"I know I'm fearing people more than God. It's a problem."

"I feel guilty when I fear people more than God. I know I shouldn't. I cover my eyes, plug my ears, and keep my mouth shut. It's easier to live in the world saying nothing than it is for me to boldly share my faith."

"What if I share my faith and then lose friends because I bring up the gospel?"

"I have to see my coworkers every day. What if they judge me for sharing my faith?"

"Honestly, I see my Hindu neighbor and I don't feel like talking about my faith. I just run and hide. I want to be different from that."

These big-hearted, faith-filled women desperately wanted to muster the moral courage to glorify God. They knew they should be declaring Jesus to the nations around them. They just couldn't figure out how to get past fearing people more than God.

Do their struggles resonate with you? Has your fear of people ever been greater than your fear of the Lord? There are no easy solutions. Yet you can learn some practical ways to address this struggle and feel joyful about sharing your faith.

Faded Ribbons

We'll start by digging in deeply on the role that glorifying God plays in sharing your faith. First, let's explore personal glory.

Recently, while packing for a cross-country move, I remembered the first time I learned to relish personal glory. My family and I were ruthlessly purging and giving away things that wouldn't fit in or be needed in our new home. Plants to the neighbors. Appliances to a sister-in-law. Books to a friend. Then one day, I found a smushed-up old shoe box in the garage, still wrapped tightly in packing tape. The box had traveled unopened through multiple cross-country moves, and I'd long-ago forgotten what was inside.

Covered in sweat and dust, I sat down in the middle of the garage floor and cut through the packing tape. Inside, the box was crammed full of faded award ribbons and badly tarnished medals, long-ago symbols of childhood achievements. Old attic smells wafted out of the box as I rifled through the awards. Most of the once-colorful ribbons were disintegrating, and they had no name, no identifiers. Why had I kept these old awards?

One blue ribbon stood out. It was bigger and more elaborate than the others and had an old newspaper clipping with yellowed tape attached. "Local student wins regional art show," the headline read. There was second-grade, pigtailed me holding a crayon drawing and this exact ribbon. I was beaming. How had I forgotten this big blue ribbon? It had earned me some major personal glory from family and friends when I was a child.

"She's an artist!" my grandmother preened. Classmates studied me with newfound respect and honor. At church, even my parents' friends sought me out to congratulate me. They'd seen my achievement in the news. Making the local news was a big deal.

Discovering this old faded blue ribbon in the attic unlocked some of my fondest childhood memories of receiving accolades and personal glory. I realized that it felt good to get the praise of others. And for decades after, I sought to get more and more of that attention.

Bad Endings

Seeking personal glory has ancient roots and bad endings. Satan sought personal glory and was cast out of heaven (see Isaiah 14:12). When Eve set out to be like God, she was seeking her own glory, too. She ate the forbidden fruit and got kicked out of the garden. Pharaoh refused to honor God's glory and was swept up into the Red Sea. The apostle John tells us in Revelation

18:7 (AMP) that "to the degree that she (Babylon) glorified herself, torment and anguish, and mourning and grief" will be imposed on her to that same degree.

King Solomon had more opportunities than most humans to cultivate personal glory. Here's what he has to say about it: "When I considered all that I had accomplished and what I had labored to achieve, I found everything to be futile and a pursuit of the wind" (Ecclesiastes 2:11, CSB).

Futile! If personal, blue-ribboned glory is "vanity of vanities" like King Solomon tells us in Ecclesiastes, then what glory should faith-filled women be chasing after?

I think you already know. As a daughter of the King, you are to be chasing after God's blue-cord, holy, set-apart kind of glory (see Numbers 15:39-41). Seeking God's glory first will root you with the moral courage you'll need to cross cultural and religious boundaries to tell others about Jesus.

In the church, we often throw around the words *glory* and *glorify* as if everyone already knows what we're talking about. We read Bible verses and sing all kinds of songs about glorifying God, such as "The Heavens Declare God's Glory." We even say, "all glory to God" when something good happens.

So what does it mean to "glorify" God?

We'll start with the basics. In the New Testament, the Greek word for glory is *doxa*. This simple word can span a variety of meanings that embody God's brightness or splendor, his great power and strength, and his majesty and honor. *Doxa* is also used to describe giving glory by praising and honoring God. Jesus modeled glorifying God throughout his life, death, and resurrection.

Jesus also has and shows his glory (See John 1:14.) As you progressively transform into Christ's image, you take on and share his glory too by praising and making known God's remarkable splendor and his astonishing, extraordinary works. If you're reading your Bible regularly, seeking after the

Lord in a regular prayer time, and pondering who he is, this comes naturally. If you're not doing these things, bringing glory to God will be hard to manufacture and sustain.

So what does it look like to glorify God, practically? I think it helps to think first about all the ways you might be glorifying earthly things. There's no judgment here. This is for illustration purposes only. Just think about all the ways people give other people (or things) praise and honor.

For example, I have a friend who glorifies travel. She's always planning her next trip. A cruise around the world. A trip to Iceland. You name it, she's planning it. I know where she is because I see all her travel pictures on social media. She's riding a camel in Egypt. She's hiking in the Alps. She's eating unknown things in China. And when she comes home, she regales me with stories of her travels: where she stayed, what she ate, what it was like to drive, where she shopped. Essentially, she's praising and honoring the most recent country she's visited. She's lifting up her travel and making it glorious to me, showing me all its splendor.

Maybe you have friends who glorify political leaders. They post on social media what they love about their favorite politician. They travel hundreds of miles to see their favorite leader speak. They make sure everyone in their circles of influence knows exactly where their favorite politician stands on key issues, and why they are so important. They give money to support their leader. They are well-read and informed about the political issues of the day. And they volunteer their time to make sure their leader stays in office. They are glorifying their favorite political leader.

Some believers glorify social causes. They're raising awareness for issues such as sex trafficking, abortion, and racial reconciliation. They put their time, money, and influence behind these causes to raise awareness, change laws, and get more people involved. They are glorifying social causes.

Some women glorify their careers. Some their children. Some their homes or financial standing. Again, no judgment here. All of us are busy glorifying something other than God in ways big and small, whether in-person or online.

Yet you are not made to spend your time seeking after your own personal glory or the glory of another person or thing, are you? No, you are made to glorify God and proclaim his salvation to a lost and dying world.

Here are just a few ways the Bible tells us to glorify God:

"Let not the wise *man* glory in his wisdom, let not the mighty *man* glory in his might, Nor let the rich *man* glory in his riches; But let him who glories glory in this, that he understands and knows Me, that I *am* the LORD..." (Jeremiah 9:23-24, NKJV).

"So then, whether you eat or drink or whatever you do, do all to the glory of our great God" (1 Corinthians 10:31, AMP).

"Declare his glory among the nations, his marvelous works among all the peoples!" (1 Chronicles 16:24, ESV).

In the same way, let your light shine before others, that they may see your good deeds and glorify your Father in heaven (Matthew 5:16, NIV).

"My Father is glorified by this: that you produce much fruit and prove to be my disciples" (as told by Jesus in John 15:8, CSB).

Blue-cord woman, you learned in chapter two that you are part of a "royal priesthood." You've been set apart to live on earth so that you will "proclaim the praises of the one who called you out of darkness into his marvelous light" (1 Peter 2:9, CSB). If we know how to glorify travel, politics, social causes, our children, and work, shouldn't we glorify God even more among the nations?

Practical Glory

Yet what does it look like? How do you glorify God among the nations... practically? How do you do it when you get the mail? While you're waiting in the car-pool lane or standing in line at the dry cleaner? What does it look like to purposefully "declare God's glory" to the nations around you at your child's soccer practice or at the doctor's office?

Here are three short stories of ordinary, blue-cord women who have practiced declaring God's glory to women from other nations in their everyday lives. As you read their stories, notice the simple, practical actions they took that brought praise, honor, and glory to the Lord.

Kate's Story

Kate needed a new doctor, so she purposefully selected a woman with a name that hinted she might be from another faith or culture. Driving to her exam, Kate prayed that the Lord might open doors for her to glorify him. In the waiting room, Kate kept praying as she looked for clues about her doctor. Walking past the doctor's open office door on the way to her exam room, she noticed a family picture hanging on the wall. The women were all wearing headscarves. A young man with a white cap on his head (maybe her son) sat studying the Quran at a table. She suspected her new doctor might be Muslim.

When the doctor came into the exam room, she made small talk. "How did you hear about me? What do you do for a living?" At the time, Kate had a corporate role in sales. Yet she didn't mention that. Instead, she told her doctor that she was excited to be teaching English as a second language to Syrian refugees.

Curious, her doctor asked how she got involved in that work. Her doctor's simple routine question was the God-glorifying door-opener Kate had prayed for. "I'm a follower of Jesus, and he put his love in my heart for Muslims," Kate responded. The doctor grew quiet. Then she surprised Kate when she admitted, "I'm Muslim from Syria. If anyone should be doing this kind of work, it's me. I wish my faith were as strong as yours." Kate responded with empathy, and the conversation grew deep quickly. Kate sat there on the exam table in her flimsy paper gown and told her doctor the good news about Jesus. It ended with Kate praying with her doctor, in Jesus' name.

"It was a holy moment," reflects Kate. "Even though my doctor didn't accept Jesus in the moment, I knew that I'd lifted up Jesus and planted gospel seeds. And my doctor really took our spiritual conversation to heart. I felt privileged to have the conversation."

Natasha's Story

Natasha, her husband, Jake, and their three children had just moved to a large metropolitan area in the middle of the COVID-19 pandemic. Between the move, working as an elementary school teacher, and parenting three kids, Natasha's time was extremely limited. As soon as they could, the family started looking for a new church family where they could plug in.

Natasha shares, "It was important to my husband and me that we be intentional as a family about glorifying God and reaching the nations among us. We wanted to model sharing our faith for our children. Yet we didn't have much time. We had to be creative. We were going to church anyway. So we decided to find a place where we might have more opportunities to cross cultural and religious boundaries."

Rather than plug into a traditional church with a congregation that looked and sounded just like them, they moved far outside their comfort zone. The family started attending a small Burmese church filled with many refugees and immigrants from Southeast Asia.

It was awkward at first because they couldn't read the Burmese words on the screen during worship time. They weren't always certain what they were eating during church potlucks. And yet they found these fellow believers in Christ were winsome and warm. They began to love the church and the new friends they'd made. It didn't take long before Natasha started leading a women's Bible study with brand-new Christians from Buddhist and Muslim backgrounds.

One day, Natasha was invited to dinner at the home of a Buddhist friend of some of her Bible study women. The first thing Natasha noticed when she opened the front door was the family's Buddhist shrine. Talk about crossing cultural and religious boundaries. "The whole experience was outside my comfort zone, and so I prayed for opportunities to trust and glorify the Lord," Natasha confides.

As the women invited to the meal got to know one another, Natasha mentioned that she was a follower of Jesus. That opened up a rich spiritual conversation among the women about what Christians believed. The women from Natasha's Bible study group tag-teamed as they shared God's love and verses about the gospel from the Bible. The Buddhist women were inquisitive and receptive. And when Natasha and her Bible study friends prepared to leave, they gifted each woman a Burmese Bible marked with specific verses to read. "I was filled with joy over the privilege of sharing the gospel with women who had never heard of Jesus," Natasha said.

A week later, Natasha and her Bible study friends revisited the same group of women. This time, three of the women accepted Jesus as their Lord and Savior. Today, Natasha is discipling three new believers from Buddhist backgrounds in her Bible study.

Stephanie's Story

"I hate admitting this, but I feared people of other faiths, especially Muslims. At the time, I was suspicious about their intentions," Stephanie recounts. "I knew my lack of compassion didn't come from the Lord. Something needed to change."

When her church began offering ESL (English as a Second Language) classes, Stephanie signed up right away to be a teacher. She'd never done anything like it before. "I knew there were women of other faiths and cultures who lived around me. And yet I never ran into any of them in my day-to-day life. Stepping outside my comfort zone to teach ESL was a way that I could be more intentional about glorifying God among the nations."

On her first day in the classroom, Stephanie was stunned to realize she had students from twelve countries represented in her little classroom. "It was the first time I had ever met or interacted with Muslims," she confided. Many of her students had come from Islamic nations where it is illegal for Christians to share the good news of Jesus.

Being an ESL teacher was way outside her comfort zone, yet she pressed on and formed relationships with her students. During Christmas, Stephanie invited two Muslims from her class to attend church with her family. She invited them half-heartedly, assuming they would decline. "Not only did they attend," Stephanie rejoices, "they accepted an invitation to church again the next Sunday, too."

One of her students attended church with her regularly and was later baptized as a follower of Jesus just months later. "Once I became willing to glorify the Lord among the nations, and once I became willing to bring the truth to them, I saw Muslim women set free. There's so much joy in that. I know if I can bring glory to God in this way, any believer can."

Glory and Joy

What are you glorifying? Where do you find joy? These three blue-cord women focused on glorifying the Lord by proclaiming him among the nations. Then they discovered the great joy that comes from sharing their faith and seeing those same women responding to the gospel.

The apostle Paul tells us that he and his ministry team experienced this same source of joy from new believers in Thessalonica.

"For what is our hope or joy or crown of boasting before our Lord Jesus at his coming? Is it not you? For you are our glory and joy" (1 Thessalonians 2:19-20, ESV).

Who is the "you" Paul is talking about? They are the new believers in Thessalonica (and those believers yet to come) who embrace and believe the gospel message. These are people in which Paul and his team found "glory and joy." Now Paul does not mean that he seeks glory from men. He is saying that the new believers who heard and accepted the gospel through him will be his hope, joy, and crown of boasting before Jesus at his return.

Can you imagine boasting about the great joy that comes from sharing your faith and seeing women of other faiths responding to the gospel? You are on your way there. It all starts by putting all your focus on glorifying God more than people or things.

Jesus' Prayer for You

In Jesus' last days on earth, he prayed for his disciples. John records Jesus' prayer in John 17. Read these excerpts from his prayer carefully and note Jesus' deepest desire.

"Father, the hour has come; glorify your Son that the Son may glorify you, since you have given him authority over all flesh, to give eternal life to all whom you have given him. And this is eternal life, that they know you, the only true God, and Jesus Christ whom you have sent" (John 17:1-3, ESV).

I glorified you on earth, having accomplished the work that you gave me to do. And now, Father, glorify me in your own presence with the glory that I had with you before the world existed (John 17:4-5, ESV).

"The glory that you have given me I have given to them, that they may be one even as we are one, I in them and you in me, that they may become perfectly one so that the world may know that you sent me and loved them even as you loved me" (John 17:22-23, ESV).

British evangelist G. Campbell Morgan said, "The deepest passion of the heart of Jesus was not the saving of men, but the glory of God; *and then* the saving of men, because *that is* for the glory of God."[31]

Oh, do not miss this! Jesus' primary focus was to glorify God first and then to save you, because saving you glorifies God. So blue-cord woman, what does this mean to you and how you live?

Start here: Notice and release chasing any personal, blue-ribboned glories so that you can devote time, energy, and effort to chase after our blue-cord, holy, righteous, amazing God. Your first focus should be to glorify God and then bring others to Jesus. By doing that, you'll glorify God.

Take the Next Step

At the beginning of this chapter, I told you that we all glorify something or someone. If you're like most faith-filled women, you really want to glorify God and share your faith. Yet in the gritty details of everyday life, you might have been struggling with making people and things more glorious than God. You probably haven't been aware that this has been happening.

Give yourself grace.

From this point forward, whenever you sense yourself thinking about or feeling concerned about what others might think about you if you were to share your faith, pause and take notice. It's a sure sign that you might be glorifying people more than God. Ask yourself, "Where is that thought coming from? What do I need to do about it?"

Remember, it's nearly impossible to point others to the Lord when you're not first awe-struck by God's glory yourself.

Dig in, stand firm, and seek the Lord hard. Sing songs praising his glory. Read the Bible and ruminate over passages about God's glory. Borrow and pray the prayer Moses prayed in Exodus 33:18 (ESV), "Please show me your glory."

Don't stop until you are awestruck over God's glory. Only then will you relish the joy and privilege of sharing the gospel with women of other faiths because you know in your core that it will bring God more glory. And bringing God more glory will bring you more glory and joy.

Think It Through

- We are all prone to glorify something or someone more than God. If you're being honest with yourself, what have you been glorifying more than God recently?

- What are your thoughts about this statement? – It's nearly impossible to point others to the Lord if you're not first personally awestruck by God's glory.

- Are you as "awestruck" by God's glory as you want to be? If not, what is your next step to seek God's glory?

Chapter 7

Hope Is Not a Strategy

"You lead Your people, to make Yourself a glorious name."

—ISAIAH 61:14, NKJV

As kids every New Year's Day, my sisters and I watched the Rose Parade in California from our childhood home near Chicago. Snow drifts would be up to our windowsills, yet it was always sunny on New Year's Day in California. I never imagined seeing the Rose Parade in person. Decades later, one pre-dawn New Year's Day after moving to California, my husband and I prodded one of our teenage sons out of bed and we trekked up the coast to see the parade. I couldn't wait for my son to have the whole Rose Parade experience. However, it was not at all what we expected.

Once parked, we made our way through a large crowd forming along the parade route. It was still dark when we claimed a place to sit on cold metal bleachers. We shivered under our coats and woolen blankets and waited hours for the parade to begin. I wished I'd brought a thermos of hot chocolate. Shortly before the start time, an unofficial parade-before-the-parade began. It was a curious sight. First came a rag-tag peaceful group of Sikhs carrying signs touting the "path to god." Next came a Buddhist group with signs inviting people to the temple. Last came a rowdy group of "Repent or go to hell" sign carriers. This group was shouting through bullhorns, "Confess your sins or go to hell."

One of the men sitting on the bleachers' front row started heckling the group of "repent" sign-holders. Apparently, the bench-warmer didn't care about going to hell. A bullhorn-toting man from the "repent" crowd took offense and started yelling back through his bullhorn at the bench heckler. Soon a tense, in-your-face screaming match ensued between the two. It seemed their anger might break out into a fist fight until security arrived and cooler heads prevailed. It was a teachable moment for our high schooler, a real-life example of bad evangelism and what *not* to do as an ambassador for Christ.

All or Nothing

Sadly, the "repent" sign carrier embodies what many people think of evangelism. Just the word *evangelism* is loaded with negative connotations of pushing one's agenda onto other people just like this sign-wielding man.[32] Many of the faith-filled women in iHOPE focus groups have expressed deep concerns regarding evangelism.

> *"I imagine having to present some long, formulaic speech that I would have to struggle to memorize along with a personal testimony that I've labored over."*

> *"It's intimidating to think the responsibility would be on me to learn some complicated method, then go out and just randomly share the gospel with someone."*

"The formulas seem insensitive. It seems like I would have to just regurgitate stuff and not even listen. I can't see how people who do evangelism would bring anyone from zero to faith in Jesus."

"When I was a new believer, I was told I was supposed to share my faith. I appreciated learning the gospel message as an outline and how to share my testimony. Yet it seemed like I would be talking at people rather than listening to them."

"I feel pressure that if I don't share my faith with the right words or methods or have all the right answers, I imagine I'll somehow fail and blow the opportunity."

On the surface, the whole practice of furthering the gospel seems daunting, especially with women of other faiths or cultures. Not surprisingly, most everyday Christians in the West think this way. If you grew up in the church in North America, weren't taught, and no one modeled sharing the gospel across cultural boundaries, how would you know?

Think about it. Mission agencies spend years equipping missionaries to bridge cultures and share Jesus in far-reaching places. Aspiring pastors go to seminaries to get equipped to cross cultural boundaries and plant churches. Suppose you're not in academia, a missionary, or a church planter, and you haven't had years of schooling or missional training to cross cultural or religious boundaries. Your church isn't talking about reaching people of other faiths, and none of your friends are talking about this topic either. How would you even *think* about crossing the street to say hello and somehow share Jesus with your Hindu, Buddhist, or Muslim neighbor? Can you imagine mustering up the courage to do it alone while you're standing at your mailbox? Where would you even start? How would you get past "hello?"

I guess if you were really motivated, you could search "share the gospel" on YouTube and find hundreds of gospel presentation methods. And then you'd face a new hurdle. Which one should you use with your Hindu neighbor? Is it different from what you should say to your Muslim or Buddhist neighbors? Maybe you should study up on your neighbor's religion or culture *before* you mention that you're a follower of Jesus? And what if you ended up doing it "wrong" and somehow damaged someone's chance to know Jesus?

"Figuring out how to share Jesus with a woman of another faith seems like rocket science," confides Marielle (an actual rocket scientist) in focus groups.

I get it. It's easy to get mired in all the complexity. Yet starting a spiritual conversation and sharing your faith with a woman of another faith isn't rocket science. And you don't need extensive training to cross the street and declare the good news. In the coming chapters, I'll share some simple, fundamental, practical things that will really embolden you. For now, let's start with three ground rules that will get you started.

Three Ground Rules

We Western Christians want to be successful when we share our faith. None of us wants to fail. So we often put burdens on ourselves before we muster the courage to point others to Jesus. We imagine we've got to develop and rehearse a perfect, well-crafted testimony. We need to be prepared to lead someone to salvation with a flawless gospel presentation (whatever that is). We imagine that we must know all the answers and be skilled in apologetics before we open our mouths. This burden is just too big and complicated for most faith-filled women I know.

We do the best we can with what we know. We...

...do good works and hope that our loving deeds will woo others to Jesus.

...drop hints about our faith and hope people will ask questions.

...build relationships on everything *but* Christ and hope the topic of Jesus will one day surface naturally.

Yet hope is not a strategy. When we realize no one's asking us about Jesus, it's too awkward to bring him up. To avoid bad evangelism, such as the "Repent or go to hell" sign carrier, we hold back from sharing at all.

Being mindful of three ground rules took all the performance pressure off me. I pray they do the same for you.

Ground Rule #1: You don't draw people to Jesus.

I once participated in a conference break-out discussion on how to reach Muslims with the gospel. It was just me and six intelligent, godly men who had spent lifetimes studying Islam, the Quran, and apologetics. They knew their stuff. They had fascinating discussions with Imams all over the world. And they were struggling because they couldn't agree upon which method was best for bringing Muslims to Christ.

I was completely intimidated. *I don't know what these men know. I can't do what they do. If they can't figure out what method is best to share their faith, how would an everyday, ordinary Christian like me ever hope to lead someone of another faith to Christ?*

The whole experience greatly discouraged me. I shared what had happened with my husband. Then he reminded me of Ground Rule #1: I can't draw people to Jesus. Take a look.

"No one can come to me unless the Father who sent me draws him" (Jesus in John 6:44, ESV).

"No one can come to Me unless it is granted to him by the Father" (Jesus in John 6:65, ESV).

"'No one can say that Jesus is (my) Lord' except by (the power and influence of) the Holy Spirit" (1 Corinthians 12:3, AMP).

Every single believer was first drawn to Jesus by the Father through the power and influence of the Holy Spirit. Whoa. Those incredibly intelligent men didn't have the power to woo someone to Christ. And you or I don't have that power either. It's freeing to know that a polished testimony, perfect words, incredible apologetics, or method-of-the-day will not now or ever make someone believe in Jesus.

This frees you up to be a normal, everyday Christian witness, one who might even stumble over sharing the gospel. If God the Father is drawing someone, your mess-ups won't matter. And if the Father is not wooing her, she won't believe no matter how perfectly you present the gospel or how compellingly you practice apologetics. You just look for the person that God the Father is already wooing (more about that in another chapter).

Ground Rule #2: Don't rely on your own understanding.

When Jesus told his disciples to go be his witnesses among the nations, he did not say, "Trust and rely on your own words to bring people to Me." So if you've been waiting until you've perfected your testimony, aced apologetics, or memorized a flawless gospel presentation before you open your mouth, I hereby relieve you of this burden.

Hold onto this truth. Jesus sent you the Holy Spirit to teach you and guide you in what to say and do (see John 14:26). When you are praying and seeking help, The Holy Spirit will guide you. He will not ever leave you standing out there alone in your cul-de-sac when you step out in faith to declare his glory to your neighbor. Jesus promises you that he will always be with you (see Matthew 28:20). He will give you immeasurable power to share. Trust him, and do not lean on your own understanding.

Ground Rule #3: Manage performance expectations.

In our microwave Western culture, we're driven to perform, and we want results...*right away.* So when you share your faith and nothing happens, it's normal to think you might have done something wrong. But hold that thought captive. It's a lie. Leading someone to Christ has nothing to do with your own personal performance. Your job is to love God and love others (the two greatest commands). So when you tell your Hindu neighbor about Jesus, you will be doing one of the most loving things you could ever do. And then—this is important—leave the outcome to him. You are not now or ever responsible for the outcome. Remember this. You can't make someone come to Christ. You don't have that kind of power.

A Forgetful People

Now it's confession time. I know these ground rules. Still, I'm prone to forget. Has something like this ever happened to you? This week while walking, I came across a Muslim woman sitting alone on a bench. She'd been crying. The Holy Spirit nudged me, "Go talk with her."

I resisted. "Lord, I can't do that. What would I say?"

"Go talk with her."

I walked right by her, hoping the nudge would go away. It did not.

I bargained with the Lord. "If she's still sitting at that bench when I walk this way again, I will talk with her then, Lord." By then, I'd hiked to the other side of the park and had managed to push down all thoughts of the woman. But God wouldn't let me get away with my disobedience. This verse popped into my mind and stung my heart: "the Holy Spirit will teach you in that very hour what you ought to say" (Luke 12:12, AMP). Oh no. I'd been wrestling with how I should start the conversation—as if it all rested on me. I'd forgotten that the Holy Spirit was with me. Had I thought about praying and asking for help, he could have given me immeasurable power to speak. I was so worried about what I'd say that I'd forgotten that I wasn't alone.

Thankfully, I'm not the only one who forgets to seek the Spirit's help. New Testament believers in Ephesus also struggled to fully realize the Holy Spirit with them. So Paul prayed that the Ephesians would have the "eyes of their heart" enlightened to "remember the immeasurable greatness of his power" within them—the exact same power that raised Christ from the dead (Ephesians 1:18-19, ESV).

I desperately needed this reminder. For many months, I prayed Paul's prayer for the Ephesians for myself so that I, too, might remember that the Holy Spirit gives me immeasurable power to share too. It gave me confidence. I pray it does you, too. Read this prayer. Then, pray it for yourself.

"I (Paul)...give thanks for you, remembering you in my prayers, that the God of our Lord Jesus Christ, the Father of glory, may give you the Spirit of wisdom and of revelation in the knowledge of him, having the eyes of your hearts enlightened, that you may know what is the hope to which he has called you, what are the riches of his glorious inheritance in the saints, and what is the immeasurable greatness of his power toward us who believe, according to the working of his great might that he worked in Christ when he raised him from the dead and seated him at his right hand in the heavenly places, far above all rule and authority and power and dominion and above every name that is named not only in this age but also in the one to come. And he put all things under his feet and gave him as head over all things in the church, which is his body, the fullness of him who fills all in all (Ephesians 1:15-23, ESV).

Dear one, the Holy Spirit is always with you, guiding your thoughts and your words. You are never alone.

Baby Steps

Early on, when I was learning to cross cultural and religious boundaries to share my faith, my husband and I were invited to a meal with an Imam (like an Islamic pastor) and his family in a tense area in the Middle East. When we got the invitation, my husband was thrilled. I was petrified. Who does something like that? Eating a meal with the Imam's family in a red zone in the Middle East was off the charts of my comfort zone. And it was one of my first experiences engaging alone with a woman of another faith.

"I'm just a farm kid from the Midwest. I have no business being here. I don't know anything about Islam. I can't speak Arabic. What will I say to the Imam's wife? Why did I say 'Yes' to this? What if they try to kill me?" Yes, I imagined the absolute worst possible scenario.

As we drove through small villages on the way to their home, I imagined snipers on every rooftop. Surely terrorists were all around. I was a mess. When we pulled into their dirt driveway, chickens were pecking around outside. From the outside, the house seemed normal enough. It didn't look like a staging area for terrorists. I took a deep breath, said a quick prayer, and followed my husband inside.

I was shocked to discover that the Imam's wife spoke perfect English. She'd earned her MBA from an American university. She was beautiful, funny, gracious, and hospitable. All my assumptions and unfounded fears immediately evaporated, and she made me feel right at home. As we drank tea and talked about recipes, parenting, and our mothers-in-law, I realized that she was a lot like me. When she dug out pictures to show me her daughter's recent wedding, I realized I'd made a new friend. As we were leaving, she asked if we could continue to stay in touch. The whole experience was a big accomplishment: farm-kid visits Imam's wife in the Middle East. It was one giant step forward toward being a blue-cord ambassador for Christ.

Shway-Shway

When we impose restrictions on sharing our faith, it holds us back. We think we couldn't ever do it. Yet science tells us that purposefully putting ourselves in slightly uncomfortable new situations helps us grow. That means when you intentionally stretch yourself just a little to cross religious divides, your comfort zone expands. When you do it again, it will expand even more. Each time you push up against your comfort zone, *shway-shway* (Arabic for little-by-little), you will grow bolder, more courageous.

Having coffee with the Imam's wife in the Middle East was a radical stretch to my comfort zone. I don't advocate taking that big of a step your first time out. However, it did forever change me. While I never mentioned being a follower of Jesus that first time, the whole experience gave me more courage to step out in faith and do it again. In time, I focused less on my perceived inadequacies and more on joyfully declaring God's glory. Trust me. If I can do this, you can too, *shway-shway.*

In the coming chapters, I'll share simple, practical steps you can begin practicing that will push you a little outside your comfort zone and increase your faith-sharing muscles, *shway-shway*. In the meantime, I want to leave you with one last ground rule for sharing your faith—grab some girlfriends and take them with you on this journey.

Two-by-Two

For years, I knew I *should be* sharing, yet it was a far-away thought, nothing more. Then my husband took me by the hand into situations outside my comfort zone (like going to that Imam's home), and he modeled how to share the gospel across cultural and religious boundaries. I stepped out in fear and trembling, only to realize it was nothing like I'd imagined. As we practiced together, we saw many people from other faiths come to follow Jesus. I witnessed first-hand how Jesus transformed their lives. Experiencing that type of joy and remaining unchanged is hard. Soon I started taking other women by the hand to share Jesus. They were trembling too. Now they're bold and courageous and taking others by the hand.

There's something special about being in a community of a few faith-filled women who are seeking the Lord and declaring his glory. We inspire and encourage one another. We make each other more courageous. When you're on the inevitable down part of your faith journey, a sister who is on fire for the Lord will remind you about how the Lord is working. And when you're up, you'll embolden a sister who is down.

Continuing to share your faith in isolation is hard. That's why Jesus sent his disciples out in groups of two (see Mark 6:7). He warned them that he was sending them out like sheep among wolves. They would face men and women who, by nature, would be opposed to God. So will you. King Solomon's words thousands of years ago still ring true today. "Though one can overpower him who is alone, two can resist him. A cord of three strands is not quickly broken" (Ecclesiastes 4:12, AMP).

This three-strand blue-cord kind of faith-sharing community is illustrated throughout the Bible. For example, Paul and Barnabas preached the gospel together through their mission trips. And when they returned to home-base, they gathered believers together and "declared all that God had done with them and how he had opened a door of faith to the Gentiles" (Acts 14:27, ESV). Their stories accented God's activity "...as the one who not only provides the original initiative but also continuing guidance."[33]

There's more. Look with me at Acts 15:4 (ESV), "...they declared all that God had done with them." Now Acts 15:12 (CSB), "The whole assembly became silent and listened to Barnabas and Paul describe all the signs and wonders God had done through them among the Gentiles." And finally, look at Acts 21:20 (CSB), "When they heard it, they glorified God and said, 'You see, brother, how many thousands of Jews there are who have believed...'"

Next Steps

Oh, my sister in Christ, I've been a part of the story of hundreds of women of other faiths who have come to believe. By sharing some of their remarkable stories here, I hope to glorify God and inspire you to further his Kingdom. He initiates the mission, and he will guide your journey. When you are in community with other faith-filled women and actively spurring each other on, you will have stories to share, just like Paul and Barnabas— stories that will change the way other women think about sharing their faith.

Start small, grab a like-minded friend, and read this book together. Then step out in faith and practice the things that you learn. As you do, tell stories of what God's doing in and through you. Sharing your faith will grow your faith. And your own experiences will remind other believers that God is in control and he wants none to perish. He has made you a light to bring salvation to the ends of the earth (see Acts 13:47). When you step out in faith right where you live and take his lead, you will change the way your friends think about sharing their faith as well. If I can do this, you can too. *Shway -Shway.*

Think It Through

- What burdens have you been putting on yourself around sharing your faith?
- Have you observed or experienced "bad evangelism?" How has it impacted your Christian witness?
- Which one of the ground rules most resonated with you? Why?
- How might you encourage and inspire others to be blue-cord ambassadors in this season?

Chapter 8

Building Bridges

"For this is what the Lord has commanded us, saying 'I have placed you as a light for the Gentiles, so that you may bring (the message of eternal) salvation to the end of the earth."

—ACTS 13:47, AMP

"I'd grown up in church yet had no idea how 'sharing the gospel' looked in real life. We'd heard it preached from the pulpit, yet no one had ever modeled it for us. Jack and I wanted our daughter to see us intentionally sharing our faith, especially among people of other faiths. So we set out to learn how."

That's when I met Laurel and Jack. They skilled-up with the basics at an iHOPE workshop and started joyfully leading dozens to Christ around their dining room table.

It didn't happen overnight. They were busy. Laurel's a writer, and Jack traveled a lot as a corporate executive. Their daughter was involved in many after-school activities. They knew that if they didn't tithe their time, it would never happen. So they blocked their family calendar, intending to engage as authentic Christian witnesses. Over time, we watched them open up their home and hearts to new friends from Saudi Arabia, Syria, Iran, and more. Around their dining room table, their daughter saw them declare God's glory to the nations. They were loving well and asking heartfelt, curious questions. Deep, rich, spiritual conversations sprang up long into the night. Soon they were leading people to the Lord and discipling them to do the same.

Did Laurel and Jack ever push their biblical faith on anyone? "Never. We started by tithing our time and praying that God would lead us to someone he was already wooing through the power and influence of the Holy Spirit. Soon we had many natural opportunities to tell others about the hope of Jesus." How did they meet so many people of other faiths to start spiritual conversations? Glad you asked. They went where the people were.

Where Are the People?

In my twenties, I bought my first car—an old, blue Nissan. And I loved it. No one I knew had one like it. The moment I drove it off the lot, I noticed others like it everywhere. It seemed everyone had the same old, blue Nissan I did. I'm sure they were there on the road all along—I just hadn't noticed. Finding people from other faiths and cultures is a lot like this. They're all around. You just need to look with intention.

One of my favorite ways to meet people of other faiths and cultures is through international student organizations. These organizations are always looking for volunteers to serve and interact with students both on and offline— participating in group activities, such as hiking and game nights. International students are some of the best and brightest from their home countries. They are hungry to meet new American friends. And it hurts my heart to tell you that most are never befriended by a Christian their age or invited into a Christian's home while living in America. You'll have many natural, golden opportunities to develop deep, authentic relationships and share the hope of Jesus. As I write this, my friend Vanessa texted me about a deep spiritual conversation she had last night with a young international student from Yemen seeking the truth about Jesus. Vanessa's not a super-Christian. She's just a regular, everyday believer who is tithing her time to expand the kingdom of God.

Refugee resettlement agencies also have built-in natural opportunities for you to serve as an authentic Christian witness among women of other faiths. That's where Becca met Asma, a Muslim refugee from Afghanistan. Over the last six months, Becca has become like a mother to Asma. "God is at work!" Becca shares. "Asma is pregnant, and I just went with her to her first OBGYN appointment." Language has been an issue for Becca to talk with Asma about Jesus. Asma and Becca recently started watching videos from Luke in Asma's language on Bible.is (an app that has the Bible in audio in many languages). Becca recently texted, "Last week when I went to visit Asma, I took my computer. I asked her if she wanted to watch a story about Jesus." Asma said, "Yes," so Becca pulled up Luke 3 on her computer. "As soon as I did that, things went crazy! Suddenly her two boys, who had been calm and quiet, decided to chase each other through her tiny apartment. They began jumping all over us while we sat on the floor. Then they wrestled in the kitchen. I have never seen them act so crazy. And yet Asma watched the Luke 3 video completely unfazed. When I went back the next day to help the oldest boy with some homework, she asked if we could watch Luke 4. Again, as soon as I started that video on the computer, her boys started acting crazy. I really think the enemy was working hard to distract her. But God won."

Linda takes like-minded girlfriends by the hand to field trips in their city. They go to places they wouldn't normally frequent, like an IndoPak market and lunch at a nearby halal restaurant. They go praying and looking expectantly for opportunities to engage with women the Lord might be wooing to himself. On a recent field trip, they visited a women's Islamic clothing store. A couple of the women were drinking tea and doing henna. Curious, Linda and her girlfriends stopped to ask curious, open-ended questions. That led to them sitting down to tea and getting henna'd. That led to an opportunity to pray with one of the women in Jesus' name. That led to an invitation to the woman's home for tea and more spiritual conversation. Every time Linda and her friends go on a field trip, they look for a free newspaper circular advertising other local shops or events nearby. It has given them even more ideas for where to plan their next field trip.

Another one of my favorite places to tithe my time and look for women God might be wooing to himself is at ethnic food festivals. Just before the COVID-19 pandemic, I did a quick search on an event app and discovered that a Turkish food festival was coming up. I gathered some girlfriends, and together we dove into a sea of Turkish women in colorful burqas who had cooked up cherished family recipes for the festival. With fun Turkish music in the background, we sat at a picnic table under a big shade tree. We met grandmothers who had just arrived in America to visit their daughters and granddaughters. They didn't speak any English, and it was a blast to have their daughters translate conversations about heirloom recipes and how they met and married their husbands. We spoke of love and weddings. Steering conversations toward spiritual matters of the heart was easy and natural.

If you're more adventurous, you can grab some girlfriends to visit a local mosque or temple. That's what Kelli did, and the whole experience was eye-opening. The woman who was their mosque tour guide had been raised Christian. As a young woman in college, she began dating a Muslim. Later she converted to Islam and married her boyfriend. Today, he's an Iman (like a Muslim pastor). Kelli shares, "It was sobering for me to observe so many women wholeheartedly worshipping a false god right in my own back yard. The harvest is really plentiful, and the workers few."

As Kelli's friends left the mosque that day, Kelli felt the Holy Spirit prompt her to linger behind with the Imam's wife for a moment. "My dad was a pastor, and I know the challenges my mom faced as a pastor's wife.

If you ever need a Christian friend to talk with, here's my number." Kelli shared her phone number and never expected to hear from the Imam's wife again.

A few months later, the woman called. Kelli met her for coffee, and they had a deep, rich spiritual conversation about Jesus. "God used me to plant many gospel seeds that day. I'm just glad I got to be a part of her faith journey," Kelli shares.

Your Mission

When you step outside your front door, intent on being a blue-cord ambassador for Christ, remember what God called you to do. Love him and love your neighbor. You will love well when you share the hope and peace that only Jesus brings. Go out your door and expectantly look for a woman who God might be wooing to himself, that "person of peace." The only way that you can discern if she might be a person of peace is when you tell her outright that you're a follower of Jesus, and what that means.

If God is wooing her, she won't shut you down. That's your cue to stick with her and let the Lord use you as an instrument in his hands. If he's not wooing her yet, you will know right away. No need to be tiptoeing around wondering.

One of my favorite examples of finding a person of peace in the New Testament is when Paul met Lydia on the riverbanks of Thyatira. Luke describes the moment:

> "One who heard us was a woman named Lydia, from the city of Thyatira, a seller of purple goods, who was a worshiper of God. The Lord opened her heart to pay attention to what was said by Paul. And after she was baptized, and her household as well, she urged us, saying, 'If you have judged me to be faithful to the Lord, come to my house and stay...'" (Acts 16:14-15, ESV).

Notice, Lydia was already worshiping God *as she knew him*. The Lord had been wooing her. Paul had an opportunity and was obedient to speak. Yet Paul's smooth testimony didn't do the heavy lifting. No, the *Lord* opened her heart to pay attention to what Paul said. Once the Lord opened her heart, she believed. And Paul was there to baptize her and join in the celebration at her home.

Shine Your Light

Here's how you can quickly know if you're engaging with a potential person of peace. Be upfront and open about being a follower of Jesus and what that means *early* in your relationship. Don't hide what you believe. You want to be an authentic Christian witness.

One of the biggest mistakes I've seen faith-filled women make is building a relationship on everything but Christ to be politically correct. Trust me, the longer you wait, the more awkward sharing your faith will become. Here's why: If your biblical faith is important to you, your friend of another faith expects you to bring it up. If you don't, it signals that your Christian faith isn't all that important to you. Your witness will be diminished.

Just last week, Meg shared this story. She has befriended several Muslim refugees through a refugee settlement organization. She's become very close with one of the women. Yet she's stuck. "I've been building relationships with these women for years, and I've never once mentioned my Christian faith. In fact, I confess I even hid my Bible when they come over to my home so I wouldn't offend them." Resolved to change that, she broached the topic. "We've talked about a lot of things, my friend, yet never faith. I don't know why I've held back from sharing that I'm a follower of Jesus. My faith is really important to me. Has anyone ever shared with you what Christians believe?'

Guess what happened next. Meg's simple question opened up an hours-long spiritual conversation about what Christians believe. Then her Muslim friend shared something that impacted Meg deeply: "Most Christians have weak faith. If they *really* believed their faith, they would be talking about it." You can bet that Meg won't be hiding her faith again.

So my friend, be authentic right from the beginning. Just come right out and say that you're a follower of Jesus and what that means. And say it very soon after you've met her. My favorite verse to share is Romans 10:9 because it's short and easy to remember. God's word is living and active. It pierces the soul and discerns the intentions of the heart (see Hebrews 4:12). Your own words don't have that much power. So quote the living Word and let God do what only God can do as you discern whether she is a person of peace. Here's how:

> "Hello. I'm (your name), I'm a follower of Jesus. Here's what that means: I believe what the Holy Bible says in Romans 10:9—that when you confess with your mouth that Jesus is Lord and believe in your heart that God raised him from the dead, you'll be saved. Tell me about yourself..."

Real-Life Example

The first time I met "Mary" from Somalia, she had already lived in America for seventeen years. She was a strong, imposing businesswoman in her community. And I didn't think she was a person of peace because she didn't smile. Yet first impressions are often wrong.

I could sense the Holy Spirit prodding me to mention that I was a follower of Jesus and what that meant. My heart raced, and all the usual negative self-talk kicked in, yet I knew I just had to say something. I'd brought a friend with me, and we'd both prayed for this very moment. Her being in the room with me gave me courage. So I took a deep breath and blurted this out:

"Hi, Mary, I'm Karen. I've heard so much about you. I'm a follower of Jesus. Here's what that means..." Then I completely messed up sharing

Romans 10:9. I'd memorized it for just this moment. Yet I forgot it, so mashed-up words spilled out of my mouth in the most interesting way. A few beats of awkward silence followed. She stared at me, trying to process what I'd just tried to say. The clock on the wall ticked. I was sure I'd just made the biggest mistake of my life. Then she flashed a huge smile and hugged me. The affirmation was surreal. She peppered me with questions and comments, such as "You're one of the first Christians I've ever met!" and "Do you know any Muslims who became Christian?" She was a person of peace, and God was wooing her. Why had I been so afraid?

What if I'd not mentioned that I was a follower of Christ or what that meant? How would she know that many Muslims worldwide have become followers of Jesus, or that she could too? What if I had kept my faith all to myself and hadn't shared? That moment taught me never to lean on my own understanding.

I've shared many times since then. Some women, like Mary, asked many questions right away. Others acted as though I never even mentioned I was a Christ-follower. They totally ignored my words in the moment but circled back months and years later to ask questions. Regardless of the immediate outcome, I've come to realize that being authentic about who I am and what I believe opens doors for amazing spiritual conversations in the future. Just today, a Muslim girlfriend from Syria sent me a What's App message to ask for prayer in Jesus' name. She knows that I follow Jesus and what that means. While she's not yet a believer, she does reach out for prayer because she knows that I pray for her in Jesus' name. And she knows that's important because I told her Jesus sits on the right hand of God and intercedes for her on her behalf.

Push Past Awkward

What if you've been in a relationship with a woman of another faith for a while and haven't yet mentioned that you're a follower of Jesus or what that means? How should you bring it up without it being awkward? Well, it will be awkward no matter what. That's okay. Embrace it and just do it anyway. Say something like this:

> "My friend, there's something I've been wanting to talk with you about. We've known each other for a while now, and I've never mentioned how important my faith is to me. You may already have guessed that I'm a follower of Jesus. That means I believe what the Holy Bible says in Romans 10:9 (which version?), 'that if you confess with your mouth that Jesus is Lord and believe in your heart that God raised Him from the dead, you'll be saved.' Has anyone ever told you what Christians believe?"

Start Conversations Anywhere

What if you need to work your way up to sharing that you're a follower of Jesus and what that means? I get it. When I was first growing my blue-cord ambassador muscles, I needed a running start, too. First, I needed to learn simply how to start a conversation with a woman of another faith. Afterward, I could lean into spiritual things.

A friend long ago shared this easy-to-remember acronym, FORM, to help me start conversations with anyone, anywhere, anytime. Each letter of the acronym represents a topic.

Friends or family

Occupation

Religion or recreation

Me

Here's how it works. You go first by offering up some information about yourself that hints that you're a Jesus-follower. That's the M for Me. Then you ask them a question that hints you're a Jesus-follower; something like this:

"Hello. I'm Karen. My husband, Renod, and I just moved here from California after God impressed it on our hearts. How long have you lived here (family question)?"

"When I was in college, I studied to be a teacher because I wanted to help people reach their God-given potential. How about you? What did you study in school (occupation question)?"

"I love hiking because I feel closer to God when I'm out in nature. What do you like to do for fun (recreation question)?"

Once you offer up information about yourself, seasoned by a little bit of your faith, then ask a curious, open-ended question. Listen hard. Don't worry about what you'll say next. Just be fully present and listen. Be praying internally and the Holy Spirit will guide you with what to say next. Trust the Spirit. He will lead you to your next curious question. Along the way, look for more natural opportunities to bring up that you're a follower of Jesus and what that means.

Diedra's Story

Diedra is a busy stay-at-home mom of two elementary-school kids. Her neighbor was a very devout Muslim mom of two kids around the same age. Diedra started praying, "Lord, how can I share Jesus with my Muslim neighbor? Give me wisdom." She sensed in her spirit that she should just be sharing her life with her. So that's what she did. Diedra invited her neighbor and her kids over for tea and cookies. To her surprise, her neighbor said, "Yes."

"She came over with her kids, and the first thing she saw was my Bible on the kitchen table. I could see that it surprised her, yet she stuck around." It was a sign that God might be wooing her as a person of peace. Diedra kept praying, "How can I approach her?" Again, the answer was, "Just be my witness. Share what I've done in your life." Over tea and cookies and time, Diedra shared her relationship with God, how he had healed her, how he answered her prayers. Her neighbor responded by sharing stories of her own, stories that seemed to be just like Diedra's. While her neighbor seemed disinterested in the God of the Bible, she kept going over to Diedra's to spend time and listen to what God was doing in Diedra's life. "I decided I'd just keep telling her about what God was doing in my life until she told me to stop." Time passed, and one day her neighbor accepted Christ. Later she confided to Diedra, "When you were sharing with me all the stories of how God was working in your life, I was so surprised. I didn't have that kind of close relationship with Allah. And I was ashamed. So I made up all those stories so you wouldn't think less of me. I'm grateful you never stopped telling me about Jesus."

Next Steps

All the blue-cord ambassadors in this chapter have something in common. They all pray expectantly for divine appointments. They block their calendars with intention and tithe their time to declare God's glory among the nations. They go where women of other faiths are and seek the Holy Spirit's guidance all along the way.

Now it's your turn. What is the Lord stirring you to think or do differently based on what you've learned? What small step (such as memorizing Romans 10:9) will you take *right now* to get the ball rolling in that direction?

Think It Through

- What are your thoughts/feelings about "tithing your time" to intentionally declare God's glory among the nations?
- Where would you like to go to intentionally meet people of other faiths and cultures? What would stand in your way of going there?

- What are your thoughts/feelings about looking for a "person of peace," someone God might already be wooing to Jesus?
- Now that you know how to start conversations with anyone, anywhere, all the time, and you know how to steer conversations into spiritual things, are you willing to put yourself out there and practice? If so, what do you need to do next?

Chapter 9

Do You Love Me?

∞∞

"I have loved you just as the Father has loved Me:
remain in My love (and do not doubt My love for you)."

— JOHN 15:9, AMP

∞∞

Let's talk about love for a moment. Good Christian girls like us know we're supposed to love our neighbors. Didn't Jesus tell us to "love the Lord your God with all your heart and with all your soul and with all your mind," then to "love your neighbor as yourself" (Matthew 22:37-39, ESV)? These are the two greatest commandments. Of course, we know we're supposed to love well.

A decade ago, if you had asked me how I was loving women of other faiths, I would have given you some vague Christian response such as "God loves them, so I do, too." And you would have looked at me like, "What? Yes, of course, God loves them. So how are you doing that practically, in words, actions, and deeds?" If you pressed me for details, you would have realized that I had no idea how I might love them. My knowledge and experiences of loving women of other faiths were non-existent.

How about you? If I asked you specific questions about how you're loving your neighbors and women of other faiths, would your answers be vague too? Or would you have a recent story to share? There's no judgment here if you're not yet loving in words, actions, and deeds. Most Christians in Western nations aren't. So recent stories aside, the big, important question is this: Do you *want* to start loving the women from the many nations and cultures who live here? Do you *want* to tithe your time, go where people are, and love them in words, actions, and deeds? If you're being honest with yourself, what are your thoughts and feelings about loving your neighbors right now?

"Once I honestly considered that question, everything changed," confides my friend Robyn. She was my one super-Christian friend who went overseas as a missionary to love people and bring them to Christ. If anyone would be loving other women well, she would. Yet when she got overseas, she realized, "Uh-oh. I don't automatically love these women." What was wrong? That's not how she was supposed to feel. Through grit and sheer determination, Robyn fought off the shame of not automatically loving others. She tried to love them. She tried really hard, yet it didn't happen. She realized that on her own, she was powerless to love others. Stuck, she cried out to the Lord, "I don't love these women, Lord. Forgive me. Help me see them and love them like you do."

You'll never guess how the Lord responded. He did not immediately open her heart to love them. No, the Lord responded by teaching her first how much he loves her.

Do You Believe It?

When was the moment you first realized how much God loves *you*? Not when you knew it. Rather, when you really *believed* it deep within your soul? For a long time, I knew God loved me. Of course, he loves me. He loves everyone. I had that kind of working head-knowledge of God's love. But honestly, I didn't really believe that he loves *me*. I think I was still somehow trying to earn his love through my good deeds.

In chapter 1, I told you about meeting my friend Miriam in the Middle East after a full-scale meltdown. I couldn't even imagine loving people the way that she did. Here's what made her different: Miriam believed in her very soul that God loves *her*. And because she *knew* God's love intimately, his deep, overwhelming love within her effortlessly spilled over to everyone she met. Meeting Miriam was a moment of reckoning. I couldn't imagine myself loving others the way that she loved, at least not within my own power for any extended length of time. I couldn't love others until I first realized how deeply God loves me.

Give Me All of God's Love

If you're like me, you've read Luke's account of the crucifixion countless times. But I missed something important—namely the outrageous love that Jesus showed a criminal on a cross near death. They both were near death, in fact. If Jesus could show a thief this much love in that very moment, what does it say about how much he loves you and me? Read these verses slowly with fresh eyes.

"One of the criminals who were hanged railed at him, saying, 'Are you not the Christ? Save yourself and us!' But the other rebuked him saying, 'Do you not fear God, since you are under the same sentence of condemnation? And we indeed justly, for we are receiving the due reward of our deeds; but this man has done nothing wrong.' And he said, 'Jesus remember me when you come into your kingdom.' And he said to him, 'Truly, I say to you, today you will be with me in paradise" (Luke 23:39-43, ESV).

Let's unpack this well-known passage together. One thief fully realizes who Jesus is. He owns up to the worst of his crimes and, near his death on the cross, confesses them frankly. While there is still hope, that same humble thief then pleads with the other to confess his sins, too. This humble thief doesn't even *imagine* Jesus loving him or his having a place in Jesus' Kingdom. "Remember me when you come into your kingdom," he says in reverence. Such faith! In that dark moment, the humble thief fully grasps who Jesus is—the long-awaited Messiah about to enter his kingdom. And King Jesus essentially tells him, "You won't be apart from me for a moment. Together, before this day ends, you'll be with me in Paradise." Thinking about this love brings tears to my eyes!

Jesus tells you and me plainly, "I have loved you just as the Father has loved Me: remain in My love (and do not doubt My love for you)" (John 15:9, AMP). I'm just now beginning to grasp the height and depth of God's love for me. It's changing how I think about practically loving and sharing my faith with others. I wonder what might happen in your life when you fully begin to realize Jesus' love for you, too? Can you imagine how his outrageous love flowing through you might transform the world?

Transformative Love

Here's a story of what happens when one new believer embraces and believes God's love.

Amie will never forget the moment she first realized God loves her. As a former Muslim living in an Islamic-ruled nation, Amie grew up abused and unloved. "My family and my culture didn't express love or affirmation. My father was very abusive emotionally, verbally, and physically. And I grew up seeing my mom struggle. I wondered why she didn't just divorce him. One day, I asked her, and she said, 'I have three daughters. I have to stay in this relationship for your future. You would have no possibility of getting married if your father wasn't present in this family.' So basically, my mom sacrificed herself for our future security."

Often several of the Muslim families in her neighborhood gathered at day's end to hang out. One day, one of the families accepted Jesus, and from that point forward, it was all the new believers would talk about. The other families got frustrated with all their talk of Jesus. Amie shares, "They said, 'If you want to hang out with us, leave Jesus at home.'"

In time, no longer welcome at the neighborhood gatherings, the Christian family stopped hanging out and moved away. Meanwhile, Amie's life without love or affirmation was taking its toll. "I had a lot of anger and bitterness inside of me. And I started to hate my father," Amie confides.

One day Amie and her sister were home alone when the doorbell rang. It was the ostracized Christian family that had moved away. Amie was surprised to see them because they had been gone for years. After Amie and her sister welcomed them in and put out tea and sweets, the family started sharing about God and Jesus. Then they said something that touched Amie's heart: "God showed his great love for us by sending Christ to die for us while we were still sinners." For Amie, the moment was incredible. She had long hungered for love and affirmation. Hearing that God loves her just blew her mind.

Amie wondered if she was worthy. Could God really be interested in her? Hearing this remarkable good news, Amie accepted Jesus as her Lord and Savior on the spot.

Then God did incredible things. "He healed my heart from all my bitterness, anger, and unforgiveness toward my father. I was totally transformed from the inside out." When she started walking with Jesus, she felt the Holy Spirit prompt her to tell her father about this same love. "It was awkward because it's not a culturally correct thing to do in my country," Amie says. Yet by now, Amie had learned that whatever God told her to do was best. So she went to her father, looked into his eyes, and said, "Father, you know I accepted Jesus. He loves me. And I want you to know how much he loves you, too."

Immediately, Amie's father began weeping because he had also grown up unloved. "Suddenly, I deeply understood that my father had expressed his love toward me the best he could. Until that moment, I had never seen my father cry. I knew it was a holy moment. God touched his heart." He looked up at Amie and said, "Thank you, daughter. I have seen a lot of change in you. I want to grow with Jesus as you have grown."

When Amie first told me her story, she had me crying right along with her father. I keep thinking about her Christian neighbors who were ostracized from her neighborhood for talking about Jesus. It's hard to fathom going back to an unwelcoming old neighborhood just *one more time* to share the love of Christ. I can't help but think how often I have stayed silent about what I believe among my mostly friendly neighbors. How about you? Then there's Amie. Full of our heavenly Father's love, she obediently crossed cultural norms to share God's love with her abusive earthly father.

I don't know about you, but I would like to be more like Amie and her fearless neighbors—filled with God's transformative love and embracing God's commands to share his love with others.

Practical Love

What would it look like if all the faith-filled women in the world right now boldly held on to God's Word and embraced God's love for them? What kind of difference might we make?

I recently interviewed Jen on a Blue Cord by iHOPE Ministries podcast (TheBlueCord.org). She gives you a glimpse of the kind of impact you can make when you cross cultural boundaries to love your neighbors in practical ways. Here's her story.

Jen moved across the country and into a new neighborhood with her husband and two small kids. Just before the move, she had completed a Bible study on biblical hospitality with a small group of long-time friends at her church. Lonely for company in a new city, she took her kids out for a stroll in her new neighborhood to meet the neighbors. She hoped to apply the things she'd learned in her Bible study. "What would it look like practically to love my new neighbors?" she wondered. Just then, a woman in a colorful blue hijab with two energetic kids tumbled out the front door and into a minivan across the street.

"Would you love this one?" the Lord seemed to say.

"Sure, I'll love that family," Jen responded in her heart.

Then she noticed another neighbor from another culture. "Would you love this one too?" That's when she first noticed that she and her husband had moved into an incredibly diverse neighborhood. "Does anyone around here look like me?" she wondered. Until this move, Jen had never met women of other faiths and cultures. She'd worked with Christians. Lived among Christians. Went to church with Christians. It was her whole world. Now she was living in a radically different world as a stay-at-home mom putting down roots in a neighborhood filled with women of many other faiths and cultures. She really had no idea how to meet and befriend the many women who were so very different from her.

For a few weeks, she stuck it out alone at home with her kids. "I had an MBA I wasn't using, and I was feeling pretty sorry for myself. I needed something to fire up my brain again. So just for fun, I decided to learn Arabic. I figured maybe I could use it." She did that for about two weeks when she realized she needed help. "Using a neighborhood App on my phone, I wrote a quick message, 'New in the neighborhood. Want to practice speaking Arabic and meet people?' She hesitated a few seconds. Was she really going to do this? Oh, what did she have to lose? She took a deep breath and hit "send."

Four women in her neighborhood responded immediately. One invited her over for tea and cookies the next day. There, she met several new neighbors. They were hospitable Muslim women from Pakistan, Dubai, Iraq, and Afghanistan. "I had no idea that women from so many nations lived all around me." During that first visit, she learned that the women were volunteering their time through their mosque to befriend and help the many refugee families moving into their city. Jen didn't even know that was a thing. "Do you want to come with us to meet some of the refugee families?" they asked her.

"Sure," she said. And within a week, she was breaking bread with a new family from Afghanistan. "If Muslim women from the local mosque are helping out all these refugees," she wondered, "maybe there are Christians who are doing the same." Jen searched online, found a refugee resettlement organization, and began plugging in. Since then, she's had countless opportunities to be an authentic Christian witness with women from many nations.

"Now, my Muslim neighbors are some of my dearest friends. Our kids play together. We talk about deeply spiritual things. I've had countless opportunities to point these women to Jesus, to pray with them in Jesus' name, and to love them in words, actions, and deeds." Jen can see that the harvest in her city is plentiful, and the workers few. "I've invited many Christian friends to come with me and to get involved. Most are just not interested. It breaks my heart."

She wishes all faith-filled women could see what she sees. "Women all around us desperately need the hope of Jesus. Sharing him with these women has strengthened my own faith. Now I can't believe I *get* to share the good news with them. God is at work in my neighborhood. And wherever God is at work, that's where I want to be." Jen's great adventure started with this simple prayer, "Lord, I'm willing to love my neighbors. Show me how." Now she's declaring God's glory to women from many nations, right where she lives.

God's Love Affects Your Witness

Could you do this, too?

What if I told you the more secure you become in your love relationship with God, the easier it will be to love others who are different from you.

What if instead of trying to power through and love others on your own, you studied God's Word and cried out for the Lord to show you his love for you *first?*

Could you do that?

It seems so obvious. God loves you. Of course he does. You know this in your head. Yet do you really believe it with all your heart, soul, and mind?

Recently, I gathered with a group of amazing, faith-filled women over a meal. I asked them to share the moment they *first* realized God loves them. Oh, I wish you could have heard their stories. They were deep, rich, and meaningful. And one person at the table was quiet. She held back from sharing. Long into the night, she bravely revealed, "As I hear you all talk about God's love for you, I'm realizing that I don't know that kind of love myself. Frankly, I'm not sure I'm worthy of God's love like that." Knowing she felt this way, how likely do you think she was to share her faith? If you guessed "not at all," you're right. It wasn't a faith worth sharing.

This is not uncommon. Just last week, I met Natalie at an iHOPE event. As we discussed this topic of God's love, it dawned on her, "I've lived my whole life going through all the church motions without truly realizing how much God loves *me.*" It's no wonder she's struggling to share her faith with others. She hasn't yet fully realized her value and worth in Christ.

Oh, my friend, do not miss this. When you fully trust and believe that you are made in God's image, and that he loves *you,* you will no longer look for a sense of acceptance and purpose from the world. In time, as you study God's Word and seek his love, you won't think twice about what other people think about your biblical faith. In fact, you won't really care. You'll know that you know that God is *real.* That he formed you in his image. That he loves *you.* And you will want to tell others about *that* kind of love.

That kind of love will radically transform you and leave people wondering what's different about you. That kind of love transforms pandemics, depression, anxiety, racial and political strife. That kind of love shines brightly and is irresistible to those looking for the truth about Jesus across all races, religions, and socio-economic backgrounds. I want that kind of love flowing through me. How about you?

Something Needs to Change

Speaking of opportunities to love, I need your help with something— seek out, love, and disciple new believers, especially those from other faith backgrounds. Just this week, I attended a retreat for new Christians from Muslim backgrounds. These baby believers were being discipled to grow in their new biblical faith. Sadly, they face obstacles you and I will never face. Their family members are still practicing Muslims. Many have extended family members whom they dearly love still living in Islamic-ruled nations. Many have families who, at best, ridicule their decision to follow Jesus. Others have been disowned and no longer have family to count on. They all have yet to find a safe, loving church family. One young woman summed up the group's experience. "I think that most 'Christians' here hate Muslims, especially Arab Muslims. It puts me in a really difficult situation. I love my family, and I want them to know the love of Christ like I do. Yet my witness is hampered by 'Christians' who hate Muslims."

If this stings your ears as much as it does mine, I pray that you'll talk about this topic of God's transformative love and share this book with your Christian friends. Together, we can change the way faith-filled women love others.

Next Steps

At the beginning of this chapter, I asked how you've been loving unbelieving women around you. Until this moment, has your love been a faint, wispy love, like mine? Or have you been striving hard to love others in your own power, like my friend Robyn? Maybe you've been loving more practically like Jen. What's true about the love you have been showing non-believers up until now?

Wherever you have been on this love spectrum, notice it. It's what's been true of your choices up to this point. Now you get to make different choices.

How do you want God's love to flow through you going forward?

What needs to change for that to happen?

The harvest is plentiful, and the workers are few. Now more than ever, it's time for blue-cord women to come forward to realize God's love and then wield it in this world. People are looking for this kind of transformative love. I pray you will let it shine through you.

> "Those who are (spiritually) wise will shine brightly like the brightness of the expanse of heaven, and those who lead many to righteousness (will shine) like the stars forever and ever."
> —Daniel 12:3, AMP

Think It Through

- If you're being honest with yourself, what is true about your thoughts and feelings about loving your neighbors right now?

- When was the moment you first realized how much God loves *you*? Not when you *knew* it. Rather when you really *believed* it deep within your soul?

- What are your thoughts/feelings about this statement? "As you study God's Word and seek his love, you won't think twice about what other people think about your biblical faith...you will *want* to tell others about *that* kind of love."

Chapter 10

Love Is Not Enough

◇◇

"Beloved, if God so loved us, we also ought to love one another. No one has ever seen God; if we love one another, God abides in us and his love is perfected in us."

— 1 JOHN 4:11, ESV

◇◇

My husband and I meet many believers from other faith backgrounds. Recently we gathered at our favorite Lebanese restaurant with Rheema. We asked her to share her coming-to-Jesus story with us. Rheema was born and raised in a large, devout Muslim family in Iraq. As a young woman, her family sent her to live with her aunt in Europe to have a better life. Under her aunt's watchful eye, Rheema grew increasingly more devout in her Muslim faith. Because she spoke English fluently, she often served as a translator among Arabic-speaking refugees. When a local church pastor discovered she spoke English fluently, he asked her to translate the church service for Arabic-speaking refugees. They would pay her. Well, Rheema needed work, so with her aunt's blessing, she said "yes."

As she began translating sermons and Bible studies, God softened her heart. She wrestled with the mighty, invisible, Holy-Spirit pull to the God of the Bible. One way she could resist the pull was to study the Quran more deeply. Maybe that would offset the things she was translating in the Bible. For hours and hours, she devoted herself to Quran study and prayer. All the while, Rheema's Christian neighbors from the local church seemed to be even more loving, kind, and generous with her. They often invited her over for meals. And hungry for the friendly company and conversation, she would attend. Around the dinner table, Rheema's Christian friends discussed passages of the Bible and shared how God was working in their lives. When they spoke of Jesus, he seemed real.

Waging an internal battle, she would listen to their conversations, silently willing herself not to become an infidel like them. She studied her Quran even harder, prayed even more. Yet all her prayers seemed to hit the ceiling. She heard nothing from Allah. Nothing.

Fast-forward a couple of years. Rheema did come to realize Jesus as her Lord and Savior. And she told me that the love of Christ flowing through to her from her Christian friends was the catalyst that helped bring her to Christ.

Love Isn't Everything

Rheema's gritty coming-to-Jesus story has all the makings of a major motion picture. As she recounted the insurmountable challenges she faced, the suspense, the drama, the overwhelming joy, I was often on the edge of my seat. Hearing stories like hers encourages me because they amplify the weight and depth of what it means to be a follower of Jesus. They inspire and encourage me to be bold about sharing my own biblical faith.

Over the last decade, I've heard hundreds of coming-to-Jesus stories from women of other faiths. While there are countless nuances across all those stories, one thing is clear: the love of Christ flowing through a Christian friend was instrumental to their salvation. Love is critical. And yet, you can't just love someone into the Kingdom. Here's why: love by itself is not enough.

I know—it sounds counter-Christian for me to even tell you that love is not enough. But think about it. God is love (see 1 John 4:8, 16). He loved us so much that "He gave his one and only Son, so that everyone who believes in him will not perish but have eternal life" (John 3:16, CSB). Still, many people reject his love. My blue-cord friend, you can't just love someone into the Kingdom because love by itself is not enough.

Caught, Not Taught

I'll never forget when my friend Georgia told me about hosting Thanksgiving at her home for the first time. She has a deep southern drawl and a flair for the dramatic. And she had me laughing so hard I cried as she described the situation.

Georgia spent weeks preparing her first Thanksgiving menu. She searched for just the perfect recipe to cook the perfect ham. She followed the recipe to a tee, except for one thing. When she proudly placed the ham on the table, she expected accolades. Instead, her husband curiously asked her, "Where are the ends of the ham?"

"I threw them away," Georgia responded.

"Why?" her husband asked.

"Well, that's a good question. I guess because my mom always cut the ends off our Thanksgiving ham. So I did it, too." Later that afternoon, Georgia asked her mom about the ham. "Our oven was always too small for me to cook a whole ham," her mother replied. "So I cut off the ends so it would fit."

Georgia had copied what her mom did. No one taught her to do it. What she learned was "caught, not taught." My blue-cord friend, I don't want you to "catch" sharing your faith without realizing five fundamental, faith-sharing actions that will make your efforts more fruitful. Don't "cut the ends off the ham" and leave out the essentials.

For years I've watched many well-meaning Christian women wholeheartedly loving refugee families and international students...for years. Love is a good thing. It's a catalyst, remember? And yet I've observed them "cut the ends off the ham" — in an effort to love women into the Kingdom, they never actually share the gospel. They never prayed with women of other faiths, in Jesus' name. They have never invited them to study the Bible. In love, they have been hiding all aspects of their Christian faith and hoping that would bring someone else to faith.

That's what I call working hard, not smart. Instead, I'll teach you to "cook the whole ham" by empowering you with five basic faith-sharing fundamentals so that you can be a true fisher of women.

Now, you're probably wondering why I've waited ten chapters before telling you how to share your faith across cultures. It's a good question. I've found it's a lot easier to remember and do the five faith-sharing fundamentals when you've worked first on your thinking. Because thoughts lead to actions, and actions lead to fruit.

Master the Fundamentals

Sports were never my thing. Growing up in rural America, I had to play basketball to have a women's team in my tiny high school. I was always the sixth player, the bench warmer. And when I was put into the game, something bad always happened. Really. Like, I would lose a contact or make a basket for the other team. Yes, these things really happened.

Given my love-hate relationship with sports, I tried hard to think of an analogy to illustrate faith-sharing fundamentals that did not involve sports. And yet, I'm smart enough to realize that some faith-sharing lessons are best told through sports. So here it goes.

In 1961, the Green Bay Packers football team gathered for their first day of training camp. In just the previous season, they had suffered a heartrending defeat in the fourth quarter and lost the NFL championship. I imagine the players wallowing in their loss for months, anxious to get back to training on all the little details to win the new season.

And yet their coach, Vince Lombardi, had a different idea. Forget the details. Lombardi went back to the elementary fundamentals. He held up a football and said this now-famous line, "Gentlemen, this is a football." Once he brought his team back to the fundamentals, he won five titles in just seven years. Lombardi went on to become one of the most influential football coaches of all time. And other successful coaches since then have gone on to copy his focus on the fundamentals.

Mastering the fundamentals isn't just for football. It matters when you share your faith across cultures, too. You might brilliantly understand all the nuanced details, yet mastery starts when you deeply understand and consistently practice the fundamentals.

So let's talk about those fundamentals. First, I want to tell you the story behind the five fundamentals.

How It Started

Almost twenty years ago, when God called my husband, Renod, to ministry, he set out to learn everything he could about Muslim outreach. He studied Islam, the Quran, and apologetics. He learned from all the subject-matter experts. It was academic, complex stuff. Renod practiced what he had learned. Yet very few Muslims became followers of Jesus. He was working hard and not seeing much fruit, not unlike my Christian women friends who are trying to love women into the Kingdom.

Renod thought he just needed to learn more and work harder. So he observed more expert evangelists and great church planters working among Muslims. And after several years of observing them, he realized they weren't having any more success than he was having. That led him to interview and study testimonies of hundreds of former Muslims from all over the world who had accepted Jesus. Through all those conversations, he discovered patterns.

Most of those Muslims had five things prevalent in all their testimonies. He started calling them the "5 Essentials." He began practicing the five essentials with intention. They were fruitful! That's about the time I met Renod.

We launched iHOPE Ministries together early in our marriage, and Renod started teaching the five fundamentals to me and to others. We all found them fruitful, too. In time he wrote a book called *Muslims: 5 Biblical Essentials Every Christian Must Know and Do.* Since then, thousands of Christians have told us, "These five essentials work with non-believers from *any* faith or culture!"

The Fundamentals

So after a decade of knowing and practicing these five fundamentals, here's one thing I know to be true: if I can remember and do them, you can too. Experience tells me that when I tell you about them, you'll think to yourself: "They look so simple." (Just like football looked simple to the Green Bay Packers.) And yet mastery starts when you deeply understand and consistently practice all five of these fundamentals *together*, over a period of time. Here are Renod's five fundamentals:

1. Love, in words, actions, and deeds.
2. Look for a "person of peace."
3. Pray with them, in Jesus' name.
4. Share the gospel, early and often.
5. Share the Bible.

Let's unpack them together. We've already covered the first fundamental, love, in great detail in the last chapter. By now, you know that being filled with God's love enables you to love others endlessly in words, actions, and deeds. Loving others is important, and yet it's not the only thing.

Look for Persons of Peace

While you are loving people in words, actions, and deeds, always be prayerfully watching for a "person of peace"—someone God might be wooing to himself. We broached this concept in chapter eight. Jesus taught this essential to his disciples when he told them, "If anyone will not receive you or listen to your words, shake off the dust from your feet when you leave that house or town" (Matthew 10:14, ESV). The only way you can discover if your friend is a person of peace is when you tell her outright (the earlier, the better) that you're a follower of Jesus. If she sticks with you, she might be a person of peace.

I like to think about discerning a person of peace like playing tennis. You tee up spiritual things—such as starting a conversation about how God is working in your life, inviting her to a Christian concert, or asking if you can pray with her in Jesus' name. That's you hitting a spiritual tennis ball to her. If she asks questions or engages with you, she returns the volley. It could be a sign that she's still engaged. As you keep hitting the ball to her, and she keeps returning it to you, it's a sign that God might be working in her heart.

Once I had a long, deep conversation about Jesus with an international student on a beach hike. Afterward, she didn't return my texts or calls. Unfazed, I continued to ping her every now and again just to say, "I'm thinking of you." She never responded. "Oh well. God's not stirring her yet," I figured. Then one day, she called to ask if we could grab a cup of coffee together. I was stunned to find out that she had been thinking deeply about what we had discussed, and she had more questions. She was just busy with finals and such. You never know from the surface how God is moving in people's hearts. It's a mystery.

Here's one hot tip about engaging with a potential person of peace: don't expect her to be a peaceful person. Last weekend, I met a new believer from a Muslim background. We'll call her Zahra. Today, she is a strong, persuasive lawyer. And she doesn't like to think of her former self as being a "person of peace." Zahra was anything but peaceful. In fact, she was downright antagonistic. She was angry at her Christian friend for pointing her to Jesus.

Now Zahra's Christian friend genuinely loved her. She would have loved Zahra even if she had never followed Jesus. And it was because she loved Zahra that she told her about Jesus. Her friend invited Zahra to church, to Bible study, to pray with her in Jesus' name. Zahra angrily kept coming back for more.

In the depths of her soul, Zahra was experiencing passionate turmoil. God was doing a work in her heart, and he wasn't letting her go. Zahra read the Bible, attended church, and studied the Bible with her friend to gain knowledge to convert her Christian friend to Islam. Along the way, Zahra accepted Jesus as her Lord and Savior.

Remember this: while not everyone will be a peaceful person, you can be sure that over time a "person of peace" will keep coming back for more.

Pray Together, in Jesus' Name

While you are loving well and discerning signs that you might be engaging with a potential person of peace, look for opportunities to pray together in Jesus' name. When she accepts, you'll have an opportunity to glorify God and lift up the name of Jesus.

Here's how simple this can be. My friend Mahreen was antiquing in a cute historic town square with friends over a long holiday weekend. When it started pouring down rain, Mahreen ducked into the first shop she could find. Once in, she realized it was a new age bookstore. Her radar was up. Could this be the divine opportunity she'd prayed for in the morning? She noticed the shop owner at the counter and felt the Holy Spirit nudge her, "Ask her what happened on July 4." Was the nudge really from the Lord or just from her own mind? She wasn't sure. Still, she stepped up to the counter and asked the woman, "Did you have a good July Fourth?" It turns out the woman had suffered a terrible fall on the fourth. She had dashed her temple and blacked out during the fall. Mahreen was the first person who showed compassion.

Filled with so much love, Mahreen asked her softly, "Has anyone prayed for you yet?" No one had. The woman looked so sad that Mahreen bowed her head and prayed right then. The shop owner was surprised, yet she quickly followed Mahreen's lead and bowed her head as well. In that holy moment, Mahreen felt prompted by the Holy Spirit to tell her, "God has a purpose for you." The new age shop owner was stunned. In wonder, she told Mahreen, "When I fell, I cried out to God because I thought I was dying. Now you come into my shop, pray with me, and tell me God has a purpose for me. Wow." Wow indeed. In that one sweet, divine appointment, Mahreen had the joy of lifting up the name of Jesus and pointing a new-age bookstore owner to Jesus through a simple prayer said in Jesus' name.

Share the Gospel Early and Often

While you're practicing all the fundamentals, look for opportunities to share the gospel early and often. You share the gospel early in a new relationship because it identifies you as a Christ-follower, much like wearing those blue-corded tassels identified the Israelites as God's chosen people to the nations around them. It also helps you discern if you are engaging with a person of peace.

Sharing the gospel does not mean you recount a big, long, preachy speech and then expect people to make a decision for Christ. No. You just share simply what you believe using a short Bible verse such as Romans 10:9. Sharing Scripture is always good because God's Word is living and active and more powerful than your words alone (see Hebrews 4:12). If the woman you share the gospel with is a person of peace, she'll stick with you. If not, she'll move on.

Recently, I had a conversation about sharing the gospel with my friend Paige on a Blue Cord by iHOPE Ministries podcast. Paige has been practicing sharing the gospel by asking open-ended faith questions such as "How do you understand God?" and "What do you think about going to heaven?" Such questions opened up doors for Paige to first understand what her friends believe and then naturally share the gospel. For example, her Muslim friend from Yemen recently told her, "When I do enough good things, I can go to heaven." Paige responded, "Wow. That's so interesting. Christians want to do good things too. Yet I know I could never do enough good things to go to heaven."

At that point, Paige could naturally explain the gospel to her friend using Scripture by saying something like, "Would you like to learn what the Bible says about getting to heaven?" Paige has learned that when she asks curious, heart-felt questions, followed up with Scripture, it shows she cares and opens doors for her to share the gospel using God's living Word.

Share the Bible

Speaking of God's living Word, the fifth fundamental is to share the Bible. Verses throughout the Bible tell us that God's Word is alive, reveals secrets of the heart, is perfect, flawless, enduring, and will never pass away (see Hebrews 4:12, Luke 21:33, Isaiah 40:8, and 1 Corinthians 14:24). God says his Word is like fire or like a hammer that breaks a rock in pieces (see Jeremiah 23:29, ESV). Reading, studying, and discussing God's living Word with unbelievers is a critical step on their journey to Christ.

Meribeny was ten when she borrowed her stepfather's Bible. Her mother was Muslim, and Meribeny had never seen a Bible before. Curious, she opened the Bible to Matthew and read it straight through. When she got to the part about Jesus dying, she was deeply moved. She didn't like how the story ended, so she read the gospel of Mark, thinking it might have a different ending. Jesus died in that story, too. Crying, she continued by reading Luke. When she got to the gospel of John, she realized that they were four different authors all saying the same thing. "This must be true," she thought. "I want to follow Jesus."

Knowing and Doing

I've told you all five fundamentals for sharing your faith with women of other faiths. They are pretty simple on the surface, right? Yet *knowing* them at a surface level is a lot different than actually *doing* them consistently.

Review the fundamentals below. Circle the fundamentals that you have already been doing consistently. Then underline the ones you have yet to master.

- Love, in words, actions, and deeds.
- Look for a "person of peace."
- Pray with them, in Jesus' name.
- Share the gospel, early and often.
- Share the Bible.

Your goal is to master all five. You can only do that by keeping them at the top of your mind so that you practice them with intention. Through practice, you'll begin to understand the fundamentals deeply. Then sharing your faith will become as natural as breathing.

Next Steps

If you choose to accept the challenge of practicing the five fundamentals, you'll face certain resistance. Look, Satan doesn't want you sharing your faith. So plan ahead for that resistance. Remember, Jesus is worth it.

You know yourself best. How can you keep the five essentials at the top of your thinking? What would it take for you to consistently practice them?

For the Israelites, wearing the blue-corded tassels on the edge of their garments was their daily reminder to remember and obey God's commands. They were constant visual reminders that they were God's chosen people and that they were servants to God and to the world. The blue-cord tassels reminded them daily to acknowledge their absolute dependence on God's grace and mercy every moment.

I sometimes wish you and I had a visual reminder such as the blue-cord tassel to stop us in our tracks in the business of our generation. Yet I realize that blue-cord reminder wasn't sufficient for the Israelites back then. And I don't think it would be sufficient for us today, either.

God gave us Christ-followers the Holy Spirit as our constant ally to remember and obey God's commands. The Spirit is our blue cord who fills our lives, directs our steps, and prompts us to realize our absolute dependence on God's grace and mercy today. He is the one who gently nudges us to share Jesus with others. And yet we can quench the Spirit within us, can't we? We can choose to ignore his nudge. We can be so focused on fearing man, raising our families, and making a living that we forget we serve a holy, living Creator who wants us to remember him and point others to him.

This, my friend, is a point of no return. You've tackled all the thoughts that might be holding you back from sharing Jesus. You've been equipped with five easy and simple faith-sharing fundamentals. You're ready to go see the people and put what you've learned into practice. At this point, you're either wholeheartedly in this journey with other blue-cord women or you step out now. I pray that you will listen to the prompting of the Holy Spirit within you and start practicing what you're learning with those who are lost and hurting around you.

Think It Through

- Tell a believing friend about an ah-ha moment you had while reading this chapter.
- Of the five fundamentals, which one(s) are you most comfortable practicing today?
- What fundamentals do you need to get more comfortable with?
- What would stand in the way of you consistently practicing all five fundamentals?

Chapter 11

Embrace Different

◇◇

"...the one who is in you is greater than the one who is in the world."

– 1 JOHN 4:4, CSB

◇◇

My good friend Lily was discouraged. She had examined her thoughts about sharing her faith. She knew all five fundamentals. And she was committed to practicing with intention. Yet she had a problem. When opportunities arose for her to practice with her new Hindu neighbor, she chickened out *every single time*. Her mouth seemed wired shut. Oh, she sensed the Holy Spirit pressing in on her heart, "Now, Lily. Say something now!" Yet she just couldn't open her mouth and bring up spiritual things with her neighbor. Why was this happening?

Oh, I could relate. Many times my mouth felt wired shut. It will happen to you, too. When it does, take comfort in that you're normal. It's just a signal to keep pressing into the Lord and growing your faith, just like Peter did when he tried walking on water (see Matthew 14:26-33).

You know the story. Jesus' disciples were in a boat on the sea. Their boat was getting pummeled with waves. In the wee hours of the morning,

Jesus came to them, walking on the sea. Up to this moment, Jesus had been training his disciples awhile. He had even given them the power to do the kinds of miracles he was doing, like walking on water. Yet they were terrified. In the middle of this dramatic scene, Peter got bold and said, "Lord, if it is you, command me to come to you on the water" (Matthew 14:38, ESV).

Let's camp out here a second. This is a lot like my friend Lilly's moment. She's been a follower of Jesus for a while now. She knows she has the power of the Holy Spirit within her. She wants to follow Jesus' command to get out of the boat and into the world to be his witness, and yet she's terrified. Can you relate?

Okay, let's keep going. Peter was a fisherman, so he knew well the natural dangers of the Galilean Sea. Yet in that moment, Peter trusted Jesus' supernatural power more. So when Jesus said, "Come," Peter got out of that boat and walked on water toward Jesus (see Matthew 14:29). This is just like the defining moment when you decide, *Even though it might be dangerous to identify myself with Jesus in this world, I trust Jesus and resolve to be his witness.*

And then what happened to Peter? Yup, he saw the wind, got afraid, and started to sink (see Matthew 14:30). Peter had *just* enough faith in Jesus to get out of the boat and start walking on water toward him. However, he did not have enough faith to *keep* walking. Oh, I can relate to Peter. Can you?

When I first started to share my faith across cultures, I had just enough faith to "get out of the boat." You might, too. You might even take several first steps. And then, if you're like most people, you will sink. That's to be expected. Instead of beating yourself up and crawling back into the safety of the boat and never sharing again, celebrate your first steps. You got out of the boat and into the world. That's awesome. Most people don't get that far.

Now go do it again. When Peter started sinking, he cried out, "Lord save me" (Matthew 14:30, ESV). Then Jesus *immediately* grabbed hold of him and chided him, "O you of little faith, why did you doubt?" (Matthew 14:31, ESV).

When you sink, cry out to Jesus. Ask for more faith. He will surely give it.

Not Commonplace

My good friend and fellow brother-in-Christ, Robin, is a gifted speaker, author, and leadership coach. He comes alongside CEOs and other high-level executives of Fortune 500 companies to help them take their companies to the next level. For years I've watched him coach senior-level leaders. And at critical moments, I've learned key leadership principles from him that have profoundly shaped my career, my ministry, and my walk with Christ.

To prepare you well for the resistance you are sure to face when you embrace blue-cord principles and share your faith across cultural and religious boundaries, I knew I had to contact Robin for some sage advice. He shared these three important things that will embolden you.

#1 Expect Opposition

When you purposefully engage with women of other faiths and cultures, you will no longer conform to what is socially acceptable within your Christian community. Your thoughts and your actions won't be commonplace, and you might be judged. Don't be surprised when some of your long-time friends reject the idea or even try to dissuade you. It's okay. Any time you step outside cultural norms, you will upset the status quo.

I experienced this first-hand. For decades I did Bible studies with friends to grow my faith. We did life together, raised our kids together, went through hard things together. We were comfortable and safe. Then the Lord compelled me to step outside church walls to engage with women of other faiths and cultures. I was so energized by what God was doing that I quickly invited friends to "come and see." Most weren't interested. Some were worried about my safety. Some thought I should just leave women of other faiths alone. "If they were interested in Jesus, they would have come to church already." Some friends ghosted me. One friend told me I was flat-out crazy.

Others have experienced this as well. When Jen began to engage with women of other faiths in her community, long-time friends told her she was "too Muslim." Jen says, "I think it's because the idea of sharing Jesus with women of other faiths challenges them." She's right. It does. You will.

When this happens, be encouraged. Facing opposition likely means you are on the right track. "Satan is not interested in the lukewarm," encourages Coach Robin. "If you are lacing up your shoes for God and getting on the field, the enemy doesn't want to see you succeed." Remember - with God on your side, you can't fail.

#2 Be Wary of the "Comfort" Zone

If you're like I was early in my faith-sharing journey, you've been conforming to the status quo for a long time. We often think of this as our "Comfort Zone" because we mistakenly think we are safe and comfortable. It's a lie.

By now, you know Jesus told you to "be my witness" (see Acts 1:8). You know God saved you so that he can save others through you. You know God is calling you to declare his glory among the nations (or you wouldn't even be reading this). When you know all these things in your soul and you're not sharing your faith yet, it's not comfortable—it's just frustrating.

"The Comfort Zone is not aptly named," says Coach Robin. "It's where dreams go to die and God's calling never sees the light of day." Don't believe the lie that it is comfortable conforming to the status quo. It is frustrating because you know you are called to something greater and you are saying "No" to God.

God will get done what God wants done according to his will and his people. And if you stay in this Comfort Zone, you won't experience the blessing of having been obedient to his calling. You will just be frustrated.

#3 Embrace the Discomfort Zone

When you step outside this frustrating Comfort Zone and begin practicing what you're learning, you enter the Discomfort Zone. This is where you learn and grow. Stay in this zone long enough and your confidence will grow. In time sharing your faith across cultures will become second nature. Yet it won't be without challenges. That's okay. Jesus is worth it all, remember? Embrace the discomfort and celebrate that you are doing something profoundly counter-cultural. You will be sharing your faith across cultures at a time when most of your peers aren't sharing their faith at all. That's what Blue-cord Jesus followers do.

And as you step out, be forewarned. Doing counter-cultural things like this will be a lot like you showing up—on purpose—to a funeral wearing cute strappy blue sandals and a white dress with blue-corded-tassels on the hem, while all your friends are dressed head-to-toe in black mourning attire. You will *really* stand out. People might even glare at you. And you'll want to run home so fast to change into black in order to fit back into what's socially acceptable.

It's true. Your natural instinct will be to run back to that old frustrating Comfort Zone where you were unaware or apathetic about sharing your faith. It's normal to think and feel that way. Just don't do it.

Stand firm. You can either be in the Discomfort Zone or the Comfort Zone right now. And I pray it's not the Comfort Zone because that zone is a fraud. My blue-cord friend, you would be disobedient if you ran back to the Comfort Zone right now. The Holy Spirit will convict you to be obedient, and you won't have peace until you are obedient again. Trust me. When you stick in this Discomfort Zone and work through it, you will have peace about it. Keep going. Jesus is worth it.

You Are Surrounded

My husband loves a good Western, and recently he had me watching a miniseries about the Texas Revolution. While the series was not entirely true to Texas history, it did give me a whole new appreciation for Texas's early settlers. There were some gritty scenes in which either the Mexicans or the Comanches had the settlers surrounded by guns, cannons, and arrows. It usually didn't end well for the settlers, at least in the miniseries. I'm glad I didn't live in Texas back in those days. I wouldn't have survived long.

God put you and me on earth in this generation. I'm so glad that we're not surrounded by guns, cannons, or arrows. And yet, we are surrounded by other dangerous threats, aren't we? Things such as constant messages that promote godlessness, hyper-sexualization, greed, envy, and strife. Everywhere you and I turn, Christians are hated, canceled, and shunned. The good news is that God is not surprised by any of this. He put us here on earth at this time for a reason. And he left us instructions on how to maneuver our toxic culture right now.

> "Do not be conformed to this world, but be transformed by
> the renewal of your mind, that by testing you may discern what
> is the will of God, what is good and acceptable and perfect"
> (Romans 12:2, ESV).

The Greek word for transformed involves a change of form from the inside out. Like a caterpillar changing into a butterfly, the word "transform" involves a complete change in physical nature. So right now, you're like a butterfly getting pummeled 24/7 with messages that you are surrounded, that you are part of a losing team, that Christians like you should be canceled, that God is not real, and that you are absolutely naïve—even hateful—if you think otherwise.

Do not be conformed to this world. It is a liar. And if you're like me and most Christians I know, you have let it shape you too long. You cannot look to the world to tell you how to think and feel. It would have you do whatever feels right in your own eyes.

There's nothing new under the sun, remember? Doing what was right in their own eyes had led God to tell the Israelites to wear the blue-corded tassels on the hem of their garments when they were in the wilderness. God gave them that symbol so that they would remember his commands and not get caught up in the culture of their day.

So blue-cord woman, how can you not get caught up in culture and transform your mind?

Good question. You "destroy arguments and every lofty opinion raised against the knowledge of God and take every thought captive to obey Christ" (2 Corinthians 10:5, ESV). My friend Robyn helps make this plain. He says, "Imagine I have two sticks on this table. One is crooked and the other straight. The Bible is the truth, the straight stick. You are the crooked stick. Lay your thoughts up against the straight-up truth."

Here's what my friend Paige has to say about this. "I'm very easily distracted. Yet what leads me to share my faith is the quality of my relationship with Christ. When my relationship with the Lord is close, and I'm in his Word, then I'm just more open to what he has for me and more intentional. So just keep your walk with the Lord firm and strong, and all the rest will fall into place."

Listen, don't be naïve. Everything is working against you to keep you living as ineffectively as a crooked stick about to be thrown in the fire. Satan... the world. They are all working against you. The only way you can make your stick straight and pull other crooked sticks out of the fire is when you realize the Holy-Spirit power *already* within you. You have something the world doesn't have. And the world can't touch you.

Take hold of these promises:

"And the world is passing away along with its desires, but whoever does the will of God abides forever" (1 John 2:17, ESV).

"For everyone who has been born of God overcomes the world. And this is the victory that has overcome the world—our faith. Who is it that overcomes the world except the one who believes that Jesus is the Son of God?" (1 John 5:4-5, ESV).

"Little children, you are from God and have overcome them, for he who is in you is greater than he who is in the world" (1 John 4:4, ESV).

"I have said these things to you so that in me you may have peace. In the world you will have tribulation. But take heart; I have overcome the world" (Jesus, in John 16:33, ESV).

Hello, Mustard Seed

My friend Terry calls me Mustard Seed. When I open emails from her, I know I'll be reading "Hello Mustard Seed." I love that she calls me that. It makes me smile every time. Recently, I wanted to try out a new recipe that involves mustard seeds. I don't know about you, but I don't have many opportunities to cook with mustard seeds, so I had to make a special trip to the store just to buy them. Then when I got home and opened the jar, I accidentally spilled them out all over the kitchen floor. You would be surprised how tiny mustard seeds are. I'm still finding them in every nook and cranny.

Did you know Jesus told his disciples that the kingdom of heaven is like a mustard seed (see Matthew 13:31-32)? Now that I've had first-hand experience with the seeds, it makes a lot more sense. Even though it is the smallest of seeds, it can grow to thirty feet in ideal conditions. That's about five times as tall as my refrigerator. Jesus promises us that when we have faith the size of one tiny mustard seed, "nothing will be impossible for you" (see Matthew 17:20).

God can use your tiny mustard-seed faith...and your crooked-stick self... to bring someone to Christ. It starts by wholeheartedly embracing this verse: "My grace is sufficient for you, for my power is made perfect in weakness" (2 Corinthians 12:9, ESV). Think about it. If your "perfect words" were what brought people to Christ, how would God be glorified in that? Not at all! God wants to use your weakness so that his power shines through you. He gets the glory in that. And you get to be a part of the joyous adventure. Here's what my friend Paige has to say about the experience.

> "When I share my faith, I just leave with a smile on my face and so much joy because, you know, the Holy Spirit was there.... It is a joy-packed adventure that the Lord has for us. And honestly, it's [sharing my faith] is more fun than some of the other things that I get involved with and much more meaningful. So it's for the joy, you know. Jesus endured the cross for the joy set before Him, and I feel that joy when I share."

Next Steps

Hello Mustard Seed. I wish we could talk together about what you are thinking and feeling right about now. Are you still leaning toward the safety of the Comfort Zone? Or are you embracing the Discomfort Zone so that you, too, can realize the joy set before you? John assures you that "To him who overcomes (the world through believing that Jesus is the Son of God), I will grant (the privilege) to eat (the fruit) from the tree of life, which is in the Paradise of God" (Revelation 2:7, AMP). Jesus is always worth it all.

Not to be crass, but we will all die. I don't want to die on my sofa feeling unfulfilled and full of self-loathing because I disobeyed the Lord by remaining in my Comfort Zone. I'd rather be obedient and let God's love shine through my weaknesses as I get out there to see the people and tell them about Christ. It's uncomfortable because that's where the adventure is. That's where the joy is. That's the Joy Zone.

Here's what I know to be true. When you step out in faith and practice the fundamentals, your friends will probably watch you from the sidelines for a time. While they watch, your belief and trust in the Lord will grow. You will discover that sharing Jesus across cultural and religious boundaries will grow your faith in ways you could never imagine. Doing this will cause you to more deeply consider what you believe. That will make you bolder, more courageous, more like Jesus. In time, your friends will see the changes in you, and some will want their faith to grow like that too. Then you can be the one to take them by the hand to show them what it looks like to love their neighbors and point them to Jesus.

Hello Mustard Seed,
Why do you doubt?
God can use you, a crooked stick, to bring someone to Christ.
Nothing is impossible for me.
Love,
Jesus

Think It Through

- Are you experiencing any resistance around sharing your faith right now? Explain.
- How does Peter's walking-on-water story in Matthew 14 resonate with you?
- In what ways have you been conforming to the world?
- Share a time when you faced opposition from friends after challenging the status quo.

- Which one of the zones are you in right now: The Comfort Zone, The Discomfort Zone, or the Joy Zone? Which zone do you want to walk in?

Chapter 12

Healing in His Wings

"And he who overcomes (the world through believing that Jesus is the Son of God) and he who keeps My deeds (doing things that please Me) until the (very) end, to him I will give authority and power over the nations."

—REVELATION 2:26, AMP

You're still with me. I'm so glad. I've been praying for you to get *here* to this exact spot...smack dab in the Discomfort Zone right on the precipice of the Joy Zone. Now it's time to fully realize the power of the Holy Spirit cord of blue within you. You've worked on your thinking. You know five easy-to-remember, faith-sharing fundamentals. You know that having faith the size of a mustard seed is enough to tackle any obstacles that are sure to come. You know that God will be glorified through your weaknesses. And that you can *never, ever* bring someone to faith in Christ in your own power.

Now, it's time for you to weave your blue-cord self into this movement. That's what this is, you know. You are not just having a "moment" right now. After reading this chapter, you cannot just put this book on a shelf and forget about it. I hope your thoughts have been changing. Soon your actions will follow.

So let me encourage you. You're not on this blue-cord journey alone. Now you are a part of something much bigger. Just by reading this book, you've joined a tribe of like-minded blue-cord women from all over the world—women who are wholeheartedly seeking the Lord, studying his Word, and trying to get better at declaring his glory among the nations. Together, with God's help, we can be spurring each other on to push back darkness and expand the Kingdom of God.

Remember Why This Matters

Remember what is at stake. If you live in a Western nation, you're now living in the darkness of a post-Christian culture. Recently, George Barna's research found that only 6 percent of American adults (and 2 percent of millennials) actually hold a biblical worldview (even though over half identify as Christian).[34] Islam and the "none's" (those with no religious beliefs) are growing fast, and billions of people are still waiting to hear the good news of Jesus.

God wants all of them "to be saved and to come to the knowledge of truth" (1 Timothy 2:4, NIV). So no matter what's going on in this culture of ours, no matter how dark it gets, as a daughter of the King, you are called to be the light of the world (see Matthew 5:14).

My friend Kamela knows this more than anyone. She grew up Muslim, the youngest daughter of a large family in the Middle East. In school, she studied the Quran right along with math and science. Kamela was especially interested in end-times stories about Jesus in the Quran. There she learned that Jesus was still alive and that he would one day return. Kamela wondered about Jesus. A bold, curious, outgoing child, Kamela inquired of her teacher, "I like Jesus' personality. How can I follow him?"

"Oh, you can't do that. Christianity is expired," her teacher said matter-of-factly.

"What if I want to meet Jesus?" Kamela persisted.

"You will meet him in heaven when you follow Mohammad," her teacher explained. So Kamela did her best to follow Islam. When ISIS came into the picture, she was shocked that some Arab nations were not cheering them on. "ISIS was doing nothing wrong according to my understanding of Islam. At the time, I truly thought they all were heroes," Kamela confides. She was confused by the disparity between what she learned about Islam and the Quran from school and what public officials were saying about ISIS. Things weren't adding up.

Then a near-death experience left Kamela re-evaluating life. She was observing too many adherents in conflict within Islam. Christianity wasn't an option for her because she understood that it had expired. So she embraced atheism. While watching videos of atheists mocking God, she stumbled across a Christian show and witnessed someone accepting Christ. She couldn't believe it. She thought that Christianity had expired. "Maybe there is a God," she wondered.

That video set in motion a series of remarkable events that led Kamela to ultimately find and follow Christ. But there was a problem. It was illegal for anyone to give her a Bible or baptize her in her Islamic-ruled nation. Through a series of stunning events that only God could orchestrate, she found her way to America in search of a church that would be willing to baptize her.

Once in the U.S., she met many "Christians" with stone-cold faith who didn't care about reading the Bible, attending church, or sharing their faith. It made her angry. "When I came to Christ in my Islamic-ruled nation, I was very jealous of American Christians who were born into Christian families. They had easy access to Bibles and baptisms. They had the freedom to tell others about Jesus. Meanwhile, I had to sacrifice everything...my friends, my family, my country...and live through two attempts on my life in order to follow Jesus. No one could give me a Bible so that I could read God's Word. It was illegal, punishable by death. To talk about Jesus in my country is like selling drugs or something in America. I envied American Christians who could worship freely. I longed to be with other believers who could worship God openly."

Despite life-threatening danger, after being baptized in America, Kamela couldn't wait to return to her Islamic-ruled nation to lead many to Christ. She knew they desperately needed to hear about the precious gift of eternal life. She baptized many before she was found out and had to flee again for her life. "Today, I'm grateful that the Lord allowed me to grow up in the Middle East and experience the persecution that I did. I'm no longer envious of American Christians. I know that he placed me where he did for a reason." Today, Kamela lives in the Joy Zone with a heart on fire for the Lord. She's shining the light within her brightly and bringing many to Christ.

You've Got the Baton

So, my blue-cord friend, I'm excited to pass this blue-cord baton on to you right now. It's your turn to influence and encourage your friends to seek the approval of God over the approval of man (see John 12:43). You can be the catalyst who helps your friends think and act differently about sharing their biblical faith.

Just this week, as I invited a young woman into this blue-cord story, she shared, "I've been timid about sharing my faith. The inspiration behind the blue cord really encourages me. This couldn't have come at a better time, considering what we're currently facing in our world. I'm really excited to be a part of this, and I can't wait to see what God will do in and through all of us."

So be encouraged. God is with you, and a great cloud of witnesses has gone before you for thousands of years. And unless Jesus returns soon, women in the future will look back to see what you were doing as a part of this generation. So let's not make this another dark age. Please don't drop this baton, okay?

I'm praying that you'll be a catalyst who influences your friends of all ages, races, denominations, and socio-economic backgrounds to join you in pursuing God, pushing back darkness, and sharing the hope of Jesus. Kind of like in *The Lord of the Rings* trilogy by J.R.R. Tolkien. Do you know it? (You might be rolling your eyes right now, and I'm okay with that.) Like it or not, one of the special things about this epic trilogy was the fellowship of humans, hobbits, dwarves, elves, and wizards all working together to thwart evil. They couldn't have been more different, yet they were all striving for a common purpose, together. That's what this blue-cord effort is all about.

The more friends you invite into the blue-cord story, the better. Look, we need each other to focus on, talk about, inspire, and encourage one another to fully realize how much God loves us. We must remember that Jesus is worth it all. Like iron sharpening iron, we can spur one another on to marinate in and do God's Word. In community, we can recount stories of how we're learning to share our faith and what happens when we do. The things done in blue-cord communities worldwide will help women grow more courageous and develop into confident blue-cord ambassadors for Christ in our generation.

Look, Jesus' disciples did this too. Sharing good news stories in community glorifies God and is a recurring theme in the Acts of the Apostles. Look at how Paul and Barnabas role-modeled this for us:

> "Arriving there, they gathered the church together and began to report (in great detail) everything that God had done with them and how He had opened to the Gentiles a door of faith (in Jesus as the Messiah and Savior)" (Acts 14:27-28, AMP).

Praise reports like this shine a light on God, his activity, and his continuing guidance as they shared the gospel. There's more:

"...they reported to them all the things that God had accomplished through them" (Acts 15:4, AMP).

"The whole assembly became silent and listened (attentively) to Barnabas and Paul as they described all the signs and wonders (attesting miracles) that God had done through them among the Gentiles" (Acts 15:12, AMP).

"When they heard it, they began glorifying and praising God; and they said to him, 'You see, brother, how many thousands of believers there are among the Jews...'" (Acts 21:20, AMP).

You may have gone long periods without ever hearing any good news stories of people coming to faith—especially women of other faiths and cultures. That's why I've tried to share lots of recent, real-life testimonies with you so that you might be encouraged, praise God, and seek to take an active role in his story.

My friend, God really is at work. He is bringing many people to himself. Every soul is precious, and he wants you to step out of the shadows and rub shoulders right now with blue-cord women who are "flinging away works of darkness" and putting on the full "armor of light" (See Romans 13:10-13).

Simple Steps You Can Take Right Now

Embrace the unknown with me and start living as a blue-cord ambassador. Here are four things you can do right now.

1. Connect to stay inspired. Hear real-life, good-news stories on *Blue Cord* podcasts. Look for *The Blue Cord by iHOPE Ministries* on Apple Podcasts, TheBlueCord.org, or wherever you listen.

2. Practice living counterculturally. Sign up for email tips, resources, and Blue Cord events that will help you keep living out the blue-cord principles you've learned at TheBlueCord.org.

3. Pay it forward. Invite ten friends to do a six-week study of *The Blue Cord* with you right now. Don't wait. You can be the catalyst that changes how they think and act about sharing their faith across cultures. For more ideas on how to do that, visit TheBlueCord.org.

4. Bring a Blue Cord Gathering with Karen and the iHOPE Team to be the catalyst for your church or women's Bible study. For more than a decade, iHOPE has been coming alongside the church to embolden tens of thousands of everyday Christians to share their faith across cultures.

Live Securely under His Wings

What rich lessons we've learned together from the blue-cord tassel of long ago! For Old Testament Israelites as well as today's Jews, the blue cord has long been a symbolic reminder to stay steeped in God's commands and stay living with absolute dependence on him. These days, as observant Jews wrap themselves in their *tallits* (prayer shawls) during prayer, they live out a symbolic, physical experience of placing themselves under God's presence and being wrapped securely in his love.

Don't forget, the blue-corded tassels are on the corners of their *tallit* (prayer shawls). Interestingly, the Hebrew word for the corner of the *tallit* (kanaph) also means "wing." This is the *same* Hebrew word used in Psalm 36:7 (ESV), "How precious is your steadfast love, O God! The children of mankind take refuge in the shadow of your wings."

Isn't this wonderful? Can you imagine yourself being covered in the shadow of the wings of our Almighty Living God right now?

I love how John Garr imagines being covered like this in his book *The Hem of His Garment.* "...(they) knew they were God's children and that like the chicks of a mother hen, they were sheltered under the protecting wings of the Almighty."[35]

Today, we, too, are under Almighty God's protective wings. And we are wholly dependent on his grace and mercy for salvation. Garr says that it's "very likely that Jesus appealed to this powerful imagery of...wings of divine protection" when he said, "O Jerusalem, Jerusalem, the city that kills the prophets and stones those who are sent to it! How often would I have gathered your children together as a hen gathers her brood under her wings, and you were not willing!" (see Matthew 23:37, ESV).

Oh, may we be willing today! This is Jesus our Messiah, lamenting the very heart of God and pleading for all peoples to come to him—to be covered with his healing wings. Just as Jesus extended healing to the hemorrhaging woman who touched the blue-corded, tasseled wings of his garment (see Mark 5:25-34), he made a way for all those who fear his name. This fulfilled this Messianic verse: "the sun of righteousness shall rise with healing in its wings..." (Malachi 4:2, ESV).

Jesus brings healing in his wings. And the blue-corded tassel he wore on the hem of his garment was a visible, tangible symbol of that healing through the Word of God. It was a very real reminder that God is the ultimate source of all life and authority.[36] In ancient Bible days, Garr says when people reached out and touched Jesus' blue-corded tasseled hem for healing, "they grasped the totality of God's commandments, and in effect, the very essence of all that God himself is."[37]

Oh, may you and I never forget this ancient blue-cord lesson. We serve a holy living God. As a follower of Jesus, you have the blue cord of the Holy Spirit running through you. And today, the Spirit is reminding you, teaching you, guiding you to walk with God, to study his Word, to do what it says, and to extend the love of Christ to others. I pray you grasp how wide and deep God loves you so that you would shine brightly and bring many to experience the healing in his wings.

"Those who are (spiritually) wise will shine brightly
like the brightness of the expanse of heaven,
and those who lead many to righteousness,
(will shine) like the stars forever and ever."
—Daniel 12:3, AMP

Think It Through

- How have your thoughts and actions changed since you read chapter one?
- What does "living out blue-cord principles" mean to you?
- How will you know when you are living out the blue-cord principles?
- What is your next step?

Notes

PREFACE

1 Pew Research Center, *In U.S., Decline of Christianity Continues at Rapid Pace*, Oct. 17, 2019.

2 Ibid.

CHAPTER ONE: WHO ARE YOU AFRAID OF?

3 Linda Lyons, *Tracking U.S. Religious Preferences Over the Decades*, Gallup, May 24, 2005.

4 Pew Research Center, *In U.S., Decline of Christianity Continues at Rapid Pace*, Oct. 17, 2019.

5 BestPlaces.net, accessed May 6, 2021, https://www.bestplaces.net/religion/city/Texas/dallas.

6 Michael Lipka, *5 facts about religion in Canada*, Pew Research Center, July 1, 2019.

7 Neha Sahgal, *10 key findings about religion in Western Europe*, Pew Research Center, March 29, 2018.

8 Aaron Earls, *Evangelism More Prayed for Than Practiced by Churchgoers*, Lifeway Research, Churchgoer Views and Practice, April 23, 2019.

9 *Study: Churchgoers Believe in Sharing Faith, Most Never Do*, Lifeway Research, Churchgoer Views and Practices, January 2, 2014.

10 *Sharing Faith is Increasingly Optional to Christians*, Barna Research Releases in Faith and Christianity, May 15, 2018.

11 Ibid.

12   *Almost Half of Practicing Christian Millennials Say Evangelism is Wrong*, Barna Research Articles in Faith and Christianity, February 5, 2019.

CHAPTER 2: THE BLUE CORD

13   John Garr, *The Hem of His Garment, Touching the Power in God's Word* (Atlanta, GA: Golden Key Press) Kindle Edition, 403.

14   Jacob Milgrom, *The JPS Torah Commentary: Numbers* (English and Hebrew Edition) First Edition, (Stuttgart, The Jewish Publication Society, 1989) 410.

15   Ibid, 411.

16   Ibid 413.

17   Ibid 412.

18   Garr, *The Hem of His Garment*, pg. 443.

CHAPTER 3: DOUBT COUNTS YOU OUT

19   Michael Lipka, *Muslims and Islam: Key findings in the U.S. and around the world*, Pew Research Center, August 9, 2017.

20   Harold D. Morales, *Latino & Muslim in America, Race, Religion and the Making of a New Minority*, (New York, Oxford University Press, 2018) 10.

21   Besheer Mohamed and Elizabeth Podrebarac Sciupac, *The Share of American who leave Islam is offset by those who become Muslim*, Pew Research Center, January 26, 2018.

22   *How to Perform Salat*, accessed May 6, 2021, https://raleighmasjid.org/how-to-pray/salah.htm.

23   David Platt, *Something Needs to Change* (Colorado Springs, CO, Multnomah. 2019) 62.

24   Wendy Diaz, *How Racism Pushed Me Away from Christianity*, WhyIslam.org Facts About Islam, accessed May 6, 2021, https://www.whyislam.org/americanmuslims/racism-church/

25 *Demographic portrait of Muslim Americans*, Pew Research, July 26, 2017. Accessed May 6, 2021, https://www.pewforum.org/2017/07/26/demographic-portrait-of-muslim-americans/

26 Leanne M. Dzubinski and Anneke H. Stasson, *Women in the Mission of the Church, Their Opportuniites and Obstacles throughout Christian History* (Baker Academic a division of Baker Publishing Group, Grand Rapids 2021) 9.

CHAPTER 4: ASSUMPTIONS

27 Shirin Taber, *Live What You Believe, A human rights and religious-freedom training* course, assessed August 11, 2021, http://empowerwomen.media/live-what-you-believe-online-training/

28 Pew Research Center, *The countries with the 10 largest Christian populations and the 10 largest Muslim populations,* April 1, 2019.

29 Taber, *Live What You Believe* online course.

CHAPTER 5: THE MOST IMPORTANT NEED

30 McNeill, Donald, Morrison, Douglas A. and Nouwen Henri *Compassion: A Reflection on the Christian Life* (Doubleday a division of Random House. New York, 1982) 3-4.

CHAPTER 6: CHASING GLORY

31 G Campbell Morgan, *The Gospel According to John,* Kindle for Mac edition, August 14, 2019, page 234.

CHAPTER 7: HOPE IS NOT A STRATEGY

32 A Barna Report Produced in Partnership with Alpha USA, *Reviving Evangelism,* ebook, 2019, 88.

33 Carl R Halloday, *Acts, a Commentary,* Louisville, KY: Westminster John Knox Press. 2016, 217.

CHAPTER 12: HEALING IN HIS WINGS

34   George Barna, Cultural Research Center, *American Worldview Inventory*, 2020-21, Released June 8, 2021.

35   Garr, *The Hem of His Garment*: 893.

36   Ibid. 1009.

37   Ibid. 1010.

About the Author

After enduring intense persecution as a Christian raised in several Islamic-ruled nations, **Renod Bejjani** (Karen's husband) spent decades filled with anger toward God and hatred for Muslims. Now he's serving the God he once denied, as an instrument of His transforming love with the very people he once hated.

Renod is the author of *Muslims, 5 Biblical Essentials Every Christian Must Know and Do,* and *The Way to Paradise,* a ground-breaking, gospel-centered Bible study for Muslims, tailored for their worldview.

Karen Bejjani grew up in America's heartland, unaware of people of other faiths. She pursued the American Dream and built a successful corporate career as a fearless, relatable visionary and inspiring coach. Now she uses those same skills to embolden everyday Christian women to share their faith across cultures. She is the author of *The Blue Cord*.

Together, the Bejjanis founded iHOPE Ministries to come alongside the Church to inspire and empower "everyday" Christians to share their faith across cultures. Since 2011, iHOPE Ministries has emboldened tens of thousands of Jesus-followers worldwide to live as authentic Christian witnesses. God is making an extraordinary impact through ordinary Christians. Learn more at TheBlueCord.org and iHOPEministries.org.

Also from Renod Bejjani

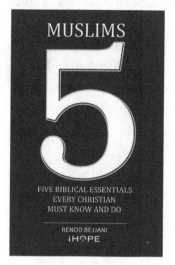

Renod Bejjani unpacks five simple actions that Jesus taught, modeled and commanded of his followers. This book will equip you with words and practical steps to share your faith with Muslims, and other non-Believers.

A ground-breaking, gospel-centered Bible study for Muslims, tailored for their worldview.

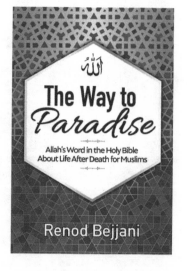

AVAILABLE WHEREVER BOOKS AND EBOOKS ARE SOLD ONLINE.